Why Women?

Gender issues and eating disorders

New updated edition

Bridget Dolan & Inez Gitzinger

With a Foreword by Susie Orbach

THE ATHLONE PRESS
London & Atlantic Highlands, NJ

First published 1994 by The Athlone Press Ltd
1 Park Drive, London NW11 7SG and
165 First Avenue, Atlantic Highlands, NJ 07716

Paperback reprinted 1995

British Library Cataloguing in Publication Data
A catalogue record for this book is available from the British Library

ISBN 0 485 11450 X hb   ISBN 0 485 12106 9 pb

Library of Congress Cataloging in Publication Data

Why women? : gender issues and eating disorders / edited by Bridget
Dolan & Inez Gitzinger.
p.   cm.
Includes index.
ISBN 0-485-11450-X (cloth: $45.00—ISBN 0-485-12106-9 (paper)
$15.00.
1. Eating disorders—Sex factors.   2. Eating disorders—
—Psychological aspects.   3. Women—Psychology.   I. Dolan, Bridget.
1963–.   II. Gitzinger, Inez. 1958–
[DNLM: 1. Eating Disorders—therapy.   2. Women—psychology.
3. Social Environment.   WM 175 W629 1994]
RC552.E18W48   1994
616.85'26—dc20
DNLM/DLC
for Library of Congress   94-3801
CIP

Typeset by Datix International Limited, Bungay, Suffolk
Printed and bound in Great Britain by
Bookcraft (Bath) Ltd

Contents

Preface

This book originates in a meeting of the European Council on Eating Disorders which was held in Ulm, Germany supported by the 'Referat für Frauenfragen' (Dept. of Women's Issues) of the Baden Württemberg Ministry of Work, Family and Social Affairs. The meeting was convened in response to the dearth of attention to gender issues we had observed at many academic conferences on eating disorders. As a first step to address this shortcoming, workers from throughout Europe came together to specifically discuss the issue of *Why Women* sufferers predominate in eating disorders, and to share their views and experiences of working with both female and male sufferers.

It is hoped that this collection of essays by women and men from six European countries will share some of the themes of that meeting with a wider audience. The authors all work with sufferers of anorexia, bulimia and compulsive eating in a variety of capacities and situations. Thus their contributions represent a wide range of perspectives from differing professional backgrounds in both the public and private health sectors and from academia.

Gender issues are explored through discussion of the interplay of those psychological, biological, social, familial, cultural, sexual and political factors which contribute to the gender specificity of eating disorders. How these factors pertain to treatment at both a theoretical and practical level is considered with contributions from current practice. The book does not intend to produce any conclusive answers to WHY WOMEN? but we hope that it will serve to generate more questions which further the discourse on gender issues and eating disorders.

Bridget Dolan
Inez Gitzinger
European Council on Eating Disorders

Acknowledgements

We are grateful for the support and encouragement of Professor J. Hubert Lacey, St. George's Medical School, London and Professor Horst Kächele, Forschungstelle für Psychotherapie, Stuttgart and Universität Ulm, Germany.

Immeasurable thanks also go to our colleagues and friends Chris Evans, Sara McCluskey, Rose Stockwell and Annie Bartlett for being around to help whenever needed.

The European Council on Eating Disorders

The European Council on Eating Disorders (ECED) is an informal network of people from throughout Europe who work with eating disorders sufferers in a variety of contexts. We come from a range of settings and professions, involved in therapeutic, academic and research work in both statutory and voluntary sectors.

The principal aim of the ECED is to develop links between workers throughout Europe. We hope by this to share ideas, to further discussion, and to collaborate in work related to all aspects of eating disorders so that treatment and research knowledge is improved.

More information on the ECED can be obtained from Dr. Bridget Dolan at Dept. Mental Health Science, St. George's Medical School, Tooting, London SW17 0RE, UK.

Foreword

Susie Orbach

When I first became aware that many Western women had a troubled relationship to food, there was no general information and little technical literature available. In psychoanalysis, Binswanger's renowned *Anthropological Clinical Study Of Ellen West*, published in 1944, stood almost alone. In psychiatry, there was only Peter Dally's book *Anorexia*. Mara Selvini-Palazzoli's work was not yet translated, Hilde Bruch's *Eating Disorders* was still to be published and Arthur Crisp's papers hard to ferret out. One read Hirsch & Knittle, Crisp and Stunkard in order to understand medical thinking.

Although many of the patients being written about were women, an understanding of gender, either as a socially constructed descriptive category or as a critical category, was absent. The transgressive, disturbing behaviours and stances which eating disordered girls and women engaged in were cast, for the most part, as pathological outcomes to various developmental dilemmas. The relevance and the *meaning* of the social and individual psychic construction of femininity to eating problems lay for the most part unexplored. And where gender was discussed, femininity itself was not problematised.

In 1970 The Women's Liberation Movement provided Western women with a new way to think about their individual experiences. Women came together in small groups, to discuss their relationship to men, to the family, to children, to sexuality, to love, to mothers, to fathers, to education, the medical system, psychiatry and work. In the course of these discussions, women unravelled some of the ways in which their gendered experience had moulded a particular self-identity. At the heart of this identity lay feelings of unentitlement, neediness, confusions around dependency needs, a taboo on feelings of anger, conflict around sexuality and a preoccupation with body image as a vehicle of self-expression (Orbach, 1978).

The small groups that women created became the space in which private agonies and angers could be spoken, the silence of individual pain could be breached and the transformation of identities could begin. Women shared with one another the confusing and contradictory messages about food, fat and thin that, individually, they wrestled with in daily lives. They disclosed how their bodies and appetites caused them conflicts. Their bodies were not simply where they dwelled but rather a focus of attention, a source of shame, a place of garnering or losing self-esteem. It became compellingly obvious that a great source of women's hurt lay in attempts to conform to the limited physical images of femininity which had insinuated themselves into their self-experience. And it became equally obvious that women, while immersed in this imagery, were, simultaneously, subverting it.

Sometimes this was done purposefully, more often unconsciously. The body became an arena in which conflicts were played out. And food, which had become a weapon used against women ('food prepared for others is good and means love; food for oneself is dangerous'), became in turn a weapon women used against themselves, and their weapon in the world. Women ate or refused to eat to soothe themselves. They grew fat or thin to make statements with their bodies they were unable to articulate directly. Food and their bodies became the text on which they inscribed their relationship to self and others.

This form of telling, a language not spoken, but written on the body, has become a terrifying and powerful metaphor for women over the last twenty five years. As we decode what we have inscribed, we learn about the individual anguish and struggle that is so many women's lives today. Where once few books helped us understand what lay behind the seemingly bizarre symptomatology that makes up eating problems, my shelves swell monthly with new books by women as more and more are able to translate from the body to the written page, and thus symbolise in less painful form, the struggle to illuminate personal and collective meanings about their food, their fat, their femininity.

This book joins the growing collection of writings which address the specifically gendered nature of women's eating problems. It gives a perspective from clinicians whose awareness allows them to understand the links between the patients they see and their own eating, between the extreme eating problems and the problems that devolve on most women around food and body image. It is important to have these voices from within the medical and psychiatric establishments. And it is important that the treatment that is offered within our psychiatric settings takes account of the ways in which these devastating problems for women represent not only women's victimisation but their attempts, all be they skewed, to exert individual authorship of their lives.

Orbach, S (1978) *Fat is a Feminist Issue* Paddington Press, New York and London

CHAPTER 1

Why Women? Gender Issues and Eating Disorders: Introduction

Bridget Dolan

Eating disorders are unique amongst Western psychiatric syndromes in that they offer a plausible sociocultural model of causation. Anorexia nervosa and bulimia are the only psychological disorders which are specific to Western culture and the only ones so specific to women. The clinical syndromes of bulimia and anorexia nervosa affect up to 1 in 50 women in North America and Europe causing the sufferers extreme distress, pain and unhappiness as well as being potentially fatal. In England reliable and replicated studies have shown that as many as 2% of women suffer with bulimia nervosa (Cooper et al., 1987) and around 1 in 500 young women suffer with anorexia nervosa (Crisp et al., 1976).

The majority of research papers and theoretical writings on anorexia and bulimia nervosa stem from the clinical mental health care professions and, as such, there is a tendency throughout these works to address women as 'eating disordered patients'. However, it must not be forgotten that the symptoms and experiences of women with clinical eating disorders are familiar to many women who would not be considered 'eating disordered' by clinical definitions. Concerns about eating, the body and self-image are intricately woven into experiences of womanhood from earliest adolescence (Dawson, 1990). Studies in a variety of industrialised countries estimate that up to 90% of women have been on slimming diets, 20% of 'normal' women binge eat once a month, 10% have used vomiting and laxative abuse as a method of dieting at some time (Cooper et al., 1984; Nylander, 1971). In fact disordered eating behaviour and attitudes are so common that, as a women, you are abnormal if you do not follow diets and worry about your weight. Women who do not consider themselves to have eating problems and are at a normal weight for their height will still on average wish to weigh 3kg less than their current weight (Dolan et al., 1987). Studies reported by Judith Ravar (see Chapter 4) show how overestimation of body size and a desire to lose weight is not specific to women with eating disorders but is quantitatively similar in both bulimic and 'normal' non-eating disordered women.

A 'normal' lifestyle requires that women attempt to change their weight through periodic dieting and exercise, despite acute awareness that the majority of those diets will fail (Gilbert, 1989). Around 95% of those people who initially lose weight on a diet will have returned to their initial weight, and possibly gained more, within three years. This holds true whatever the means of dieting (Garner and Wooley, 1991). The dieting industry remains one of the more lucrative areas to be in, despite the fact that its success is built upon its customers' failure.

A popular opinion of anorexia nervosa and bulimia nervosa is that they are 'slimmer's diseases' – a vain woman's attempt to be beautiful – with such a view propagated by the media it is not surprising that many non-sufferers are intolerant of their friend's or daughter's lack of ability to stop their disordered eating behaviours. This simplistic and incorrect interpretation of eating disorders does not give sufficient credence to the variety factors which combine to produce and maintain a disordered relationship with food. Clinical explanations of anorexia and bulimia nervosa are most often focussed on the individual patient, but to understand the development of eating disorders in the individual woman the disorder must be placed within a societal context. A range of sociocultural, familial, psychological and political pressures impact upon women and have contributed to the current proliferation of eating problems.

The positive valuation of slimness is an extremely recent development in our culture. Earliest representations of women were corpulent and fertility was the main consideration, as perhaps best exemplified in the 'Venus von Willendorf' a 25,000 year old Stone Age figure from Austria which is a woman who consists of large breasts, stomach, hips, thighs, and buttocks, but has no face. Through Raphael and Rubens the fuller rounded figure maintained an image of voluptuous femininity. However with the Romantic movement a new standard of beauty began to emerge. Individualism, creativity and passion, were promoted and by the nineteenth century a consumptive image, of thinness and pale skin was lauded in women and men. Perhaps coincidentally in England and France the medical journals of the 1870's carried first descriptions of a hitherto unrecognised syndrome 'anorexia nervosa (hysterica)' (Gull, 1874).

In the society of the 1920s the 'flapper' look appeared, a fashion which required women to forgo any curves or breasts which may reveal their femininity and fertility. This more asexual image for women developed after a World War, at a time of increased social status and some economic freedom for women. A 1927 book on 'Girlhood and Wifehood' described how the social position of women was changing at this time –

'Time was when the majority of young women looked forward to nothing better than being a housewife and a wifely comforter and help of the man she loved. Alas! we have changed all that. The exigencies of life have pressed women into the arena of strife and they now compete with men for the means of existence' (p.7. Anon, 1927).

Although thinness was in vogue through the 1920–30s there is little evidence of a major increase in eating disorders, however it has been suggested that this is because when anorexia nervosa did develop it was often mistakenly viewed as a biological endocrine disorder (Simmonds Disease) which was then treated with thyroid extracts.

By the post-war years breasts and curves returned and the beauty ideals of the era are epitomised in Marilyn Monroe, who at size 16, would never make it as a supermodel or beauty icon today. In Chapter 5, Glen Waller and Julie Shaw discuss how powerful today's media images of women are in conveying the socio- cultural ideals of thinness. Many commentators have linked the development of anorexia nervosa to the sexual and political revolutions of the 1960's. Certainly the flapper's straight asexual style was re-echoed in the 1960's and in tandem came the beginnings of the eating disorders epidemic.

However, to simply recount our changing fashions does not

elucidate the meanings of thinness for women. One obvious connection is that between fatness and fertility. Fatness represents both wealth and the ability to nurture, to have children. In some East and Central African countries 'fattening sheds' are still used where girls at the time of puberty are overfed and have their bodies displayed in a ceremony to signify their reproductive and economic status. In such societies fatness remains valued over slimness, at least for women, and cases of anorexia and bulimia are extremely rare (Dolan, 1991). However, even in those cultures which deplore thinness, women are not immune to eating problems and the societal valuation of excessive weight brings its own dilemmas for women. Toubia (1988) discusses how for Sudanese Arab women the overvaluation of fatness, combined with a lack of exercise and sporting activity due to social restrictions, produces an excessively high weight for women which is far above limits for a healthy body. She describes how successful wives are those who prepare rich diverse meals and entertain and that this overemphasis on food consumes womens' mental and physical energy leaving little time for cultural social and political activities. Toubia reports that compulsive eating is frequently displayed by Arab women as a symptom of their frustration and depression.

One view of the Western trend away from fatness is that this represents a statement that women should no longer be valued only for their fertility or ability to reproduce. That a woman's body should no longer be used to signify that someone else (her father, husband or brother) is strong and rich enough to provide for and feed her. It can not be completely coincidental that trends of idealisation of thinness in the 1920's and 1960's developed in parallel with the emancipation of women and sexual liberation in the West.

These changes in the socio-political position of women have come at a time when our society has become more affluent. Standards of living have improved rapidly, food is in abundance and less people do physical labour. There is plenty of evidence that women and men have grown fatter over the last decades. Only in such a social situation where over-consumption is possible, or even too easy, can slimming become seen as a luxury and a desirable activity.

However, there is a paradox in describing this move away from fatness as a symbol of womens' freedom. The thin shape we are now asked to conform to also disempowers women. It is not the shape of a strong adult, but of a weak powerless child, no curves or

breasts, but an asexual, infertile, hair-free adolescent. Naomi Wolf
has described dieting as 'the most potent political sedative in
women's history'. She describes the drive for thinness not as an
obsession with female beauty but as an obsession with female
obedience (Wolf, 1990).

An important aspect of this socio-cultural position of women
which may contribute to eating disorders is the conflicting roles
which our society asks adult women to fulfill. Concepts of feminine
beauty conflict with the modern idea of thinness as a symbol of
social and sexual freedom to produce contradictory role definitions
for women. Winny Weeda-Mannak (in Chapter 2), outlines how
specific sex-role pressures upon women, may influence the development of eating disorders. Western societies are characterised by
increasing individualisation and the primacy of the 'self'. People
are required to develop their own individual identity, opinions and
needs. However for women this brings a plethora of confusing role
expectations. The number of possible roles for women have ex-
panded both in the home and in the public domain. We all now
recognise the 'Superwoman' syndrome. A woman is expected to be
a mother, have a career, be a dutiful wife, an exciting mistress, be
romantic but also be independent – and stay in control of all of
this. Selvini-Palazzoli (1985) described the modern woman as
having to 'put away her hard earned diplomas and wash the
nappies'. Women are now supposed to have all the traditional
feminine traits but traditional masculine characteristics too. The
position is impossible. No one woman can fulfill all of these roles
perfectly, but we are made to feel a failure if we do not meet them.
The striving for perfection and control is intensified. Many women
do manage to juggle the different parts of their lives, but often at
the expense of ignoring their own needs.

This does not mean that if women had these new possibilities
and independence taken away, and were put back in the kitchen,
we would all be happy and stress free. At the moment the position
seems to be rather 'all or nothing'. If a woman chooses to be a
mother at home she is made to feel inadequate for not making
enough of her life and having a job outside the home. If a woman
puts her career first and chooses not to have children she is seen as
an incomplete woman, people question why she does not have a
partner. You do not often hear people publicly question why a
man does not have a child, or ask him if he feels incomplete

without a wife. Women are not yet in the position of men, who are presented with several alternative but equal choices. At the same time we are in a world where whichever role you may take the first priority for every woman is to look good.

It is not surprising then that women learn to cling to that one point when other things are impossible to control, and seek at least to control their own bodies believing that if that one thing was perfect the rest would follow. Weight control has becomes women's substitute for effective control of their lives. But this search for control through dieting is fated. Diets inevitably fail and the dieter will not always conquer her hunger, instead she will experience even greater loss of control.

Placing such an emphasis upon the socio-cultural context need not necessarily deny that biological factors have a part to play in the development of eating disorders. Studies of twins, who share identical genetic make-up, have shown a higher concordance for eating disorders than expected by chance. Genetically inherited factors may predetermine an individual's shape, body weight, physical features, metabolic rate, hormonal balance, the timing of puberty and menarche etc. but, as yet, no biological factor has been identified which predetermines the development of an eating disorder. It seems unlikely that any such feature or combination of features will ever be found in isolation from the societal context. However, when a genetic predisposition, such as being naturally larger than ones peers, coincides with the Western socio-cultural pressure on women to feel 'abnormal' and 'fat' if overweight it is easier to see how the cultural meaning of this biologically determined state may push a woman to try and manipulate her weight and fight against her biology.

Various common familial factors have been described in women who develop eating problems. Higher parental age, parental marital problems, psychological problems in individual parents such as alcoholic fathers and depressed mothers are often reported. Women with bulimia report repressive sexual attitudes in their families, inability to communicate with their parents, not being understood by their parents (Kog & Vandereycken, 1985; Dolan et al., 1990). In Chapter 3, Karin Bell highlights aspects of the mother-daughter relationship which can contribute to the development of bulimia.

The symbolic meanings of bulimia and food for women, both as individuals and as family members have already been well described

(Chernin, 1986; Edwards, 1987). Eating is a biological necessity, but included amongst its symbolic function, are sexuality, social status, nurturance and care (Greenaway, 1990; Lawrence, 1987). In childhood, physical and emotional care are embodied in being fed by another person, usually a woman. Abuse of food can be seen to symbolise dissatisfaction with this nurturance and, when the abuse is either the restriction of anorexia nervosa or the over-eating in bulimia and obesity, the communication can be very powerful. Refusal of food from the parents can indicate the child's rejection of the parent's overintrusive need to care for them; overeating, or comfort eating, can be a substitute for the care and attention which a person may feel she needs but which is either not available, or is refused. The woman with an eating problem experiences emotional disturbance but may have no way to express her distress verbally. Instead, the emotional turmoil is translated into the behavioural symptoms of starvation, binge eating or vomiting. However, food abuse itself leads to distressing feelings of guilt, shame and disgust, thereby setting up a vicious cycle of negative emotions.

Eating problems often develop in the mid teenage years, at a time when women are making the transition from child to adult, they are beginning to form their first sexual relationships and the socio-culturally determined valuation of female body shape acquires a personal relevance. A woman who has turned to food for comfort and psychological nurture is now faced with a dilemma. Food had been her source of emotional support but now the weight and body shape that result from over-eating are contrary to prevailing socio-cultural ideals. A major conflict now exists which can apparently only be resolved by eating excessively but using some measure to prevent weight gain – the resolution is bulimia or anorexia nervosa.

Although one can suggest such summaries of familial contribution to eating disorders, it is clear that the diversity of the family experiences of women is in great contrast to the uniformity of the age of onset of eating problems (in adolescence and early adulthood) and the remarkable preponderance of female over male sufferers. Any attempt to explain eating disorders should begin with these striking regularities. People with familial stressors can develop a range of different psychological problems. So we need to ask why does a particular person develop an eating problem rather than any other. And we must remember that the 'person' we are talking about is a woman.

Given the plethora of recent publications and interest in sexual abuse it is almost inevitable that connections between abusive sexual experiences and eating disorders have been explored. Incidence of sexual victimisation of children and adults is increasing and we know that female children are at three times greater risk than boys of sexual victimisation (Finkelhor, 1979). Chapter 11, by Rachel Calam and Peter Slade, highlights how we are only just beginning to understand the importance of adverse sexual experiences for women and whether certain events are specific to the development of eating disorders. Dealing with sexual issues and conflicts is an essential part of therapy in eating disorders. Ellie van Vreckem and Walter Vandereycken, in Chapter 12 describe a therapeutic model devised in Belgium in which women with eating disorders share their experiences of sexual trauma and discuss sexual issues together within a special group programme.

An important aspect of helping women overcome their eating problems, which is given space in this volume, is sharing experiences with other women. This can be in the community self-help group (Chapter 8); in group psychotherapy (Chapter 10); as a component of a wider clinical therapy programme (Chapters 9, 12); or perhaps in individual therapy with a woman therapist. It is a continuing debate whether only women therapists should have exclusive involvement in women's problems. Rose Stockwell (Chapter 6) considers the gender of the therapist and asks what might contribute to the preferability of women for treating women with eating disorders. However at the present time in most statutory sector (medical) treatment settings the consultant in charge (and possibly the therapist) will be male. Werner Köpp (Chapter 7) puts forward some of the arguments for why men can also be successful therapists.

Although the focus in this book is on women it should not be forgotten that a minority of men also suffer from eating disorders. Any attempt to understand the gender imbalance of eating disorders must include men's experiences. Pat Hartley describes in Chapter 13 how the inclusion of men in community self-help groups (as sufferers, relatives or friends) can enrich the experience of the women in the group whilst for male patients, relatives and therapists the predominantly female group provides a forum to increase their own understanding of women's experiences.

Rachel Bryant-Waugh in Chapter 14 notes how in young anorectics the male-female ratio is much higher than that found in adolescents and adults. She contends that the role of gender is less central to the development of eating disorders in children than in older age groups. Perhaps we should ask what happens in the continuing socialisation of women which swings the balance so far to the extreme?

A particular difficulty for women and men workers in this area is the extent to which their own social, personal and political positions influence the generation of research and clinical questions. Of necessity this volume represents a highly selective sample of views and issues within the current field of eating disorders work. The title of this book is posed as a question, WHY WOMEN?, yet the contributions are intended to generate more questions than can be answered. Many points made will be theoretical and contentious, all have arguments for and against them.

To only concentrate on women's social-political positions and the slimness and dieting culture will not provide a total explanation for the development of clinical eating disorders. Other factors familial, individual psychological and biological play a part. The etiology of eating problems is complex and no one single causal factor has been, or ever will be, identified. Socio-cultural factors are a necessary, but not sufficient determinant of eating disorder. Critics of socio-cultural models will say that they explain very little as not all women exposed to these societal ideals have an eating disorder and that men can have eating disorders too. However it seems that almost all women in our society do have a 'disordered' relationship with food and bodies, even though we may not all be clinical cases coming to see doctors.

Perhaps the question WHY WOMEN? will never be satisfactorily answered. However what has been missing in the clinical literature is not simply the answers, but the discourse, the awareness of how one should form the questions and what those questions are. Edwards (1987) has emphasised how no-one should attempt to understand the psychology of eating problems without considering the wider social context. To do so 'would be to fall into the trap which ensnares so many 'neurotic' women: to locate the source of all their problems within themselves, and thus seek exclusively intrapersonal change'. Eating disorders have previously been presented as a disorder of women, but perhaps we could ask if they are actually a disorder of our culture?

REFERENCES

Anon (1927) *Girlhood and Wifehood: Practical Counsel and Advice.* London, Clarke Son & Platt Ltd.

Chernin K. (1986) *The hungry self: Women, eating and identity.* London, Virago Press Ltd.

Cooper P., Charnock D. & Taylor M. (1987) The prevalence of bulimia nervosa: A replication study. *British Journal of Psychiatry,* 151: 684–686.

Crisp A., Palmer R. & Kalucy R. (1976) How common is anorexia nervosa? A prevalence study. *British Journal of Psychiatry,* 128: 549–554

Dawson J. (1990) *How do I look?* London, Virago Press Ltd.

Dolan B., Lieberman S., Lacey J.H. & Evans C. (1990) Family features associated with normal body weight bulimia. *International Journal of Eating Disorders,* vol. 9(6): 638–647

Dolan B. (1991) Cross cultural aspects of anorexia nervosa and bulimia nervosa: A review. *International Journal of Eating Disorders,* vol. 10(1): 67–69

Dolan B., Birtchnell S., Lacey J.H. (1987) Body image distortion in non-eating disordered women and men. *Journal of Psychosomatic Research,* 31(4): 513–520

Edwards G (1987) Anorexia and the family – in Lawrence M. (op. cit.)

Finkelhor D (1979) *Sexually victimised children.* Glencoe, USA; Free Press.

Garner D.M., Wooley S (1991) Confronting the failure of behavioural and dietary treatments for obesity. *Clinical Psychology Review,* 11: 729–780.

Greenaway P (1990) *The cook, the thief, his wife and her lover.* London, Palace Pictures.

Gilbert S. (1989) *Tomorrow I'll be slim: The psychology of dieting.* London, Routledge

Gull W.W. (1874) Anorexia nervosa (apepsia hysterica, anorexia hysterica). *Transactions of the Clinical Society,* London, 7: 22, report on a paper read in October 1873.

Kog E. & Vandereycken W. (1985) Family characteristics of anorexia nervosa and bulimia: A review of the reserach literature. *Clinical Psychology Review,* 5: 159–180

Lawrence M. (ed) *Fed up and hungry: Women, oppression and food,* London, Women's Press Ltd.

Nylander I. (1971) The feeling of being fat and dieting in a school population. *Acta Socio-Medica Scandanavica,* 1: 17–26

Selvini-Palazzoli M. (1985) Anorexia nervosa: A syndrome of the affluent society. *Transcultural Psychiatric Research Review,* 22: 199–205.

Toubia N (1988) *Women of the Arab World*. London, Zed Books.
Wolf N. (1990) *The Beauty Myth*. London, Chatto & Windus

SOCIO-CULTURAL ASPECTS

CHAPTER 2

Female Sex-role Conflicts and Eating Disorders

Winny Weeda-Mannak

Clinical as well as epidemiological studies have shown that eating disorders occur more commonly in females than males, usually developing around puberty and adolescence. The evidence that anorexia and bulimia nervosa are more common in females has resulted in the postulation that socio-cultural factors may be important determinants in the onset of anorexia and bulimia nervosa. The purpose of this chapter is to highlight the socio-cultural variables considered to contribute to the expression of anorexia or bulimia nervosa in women.

CONTEMPORARY SYMBOLS OF FASHION

Concepts of feminine beauty have varied through history. Throughout centuries different body shapes have been selected for, and associated with, desirable social virtues (Schwartz & Thompson, 1980). During the last decades a shift towards leanness and thinness for women could be observed in Western societies and has been linked to an increase in the prevalence of eating disorders (Selvini-Palazzoli, 1974; Boskind-Lodahl, 1976; Bruch, 1978). Ryle (1939) probably was the first to emphasise that the social pressure of the slimming fashion may provide a general increase of anorexia nervosa. Also Bruch (1978) has referred to the increase of anorexia nervosa as 'an epidemic illness the spread of which may be attributed to psycho- sociological factors'. The change of idealised female shape has been documented and quantified in a study by Garner et al. (1980). The authors collected data on body weight and height from several sources including Playboy Magazine and Miss America Pageants. One may conclude from their data that thinness had been valued as a symbol of beauty as well as of sexual attractiveness. The cultural pressure to be thin, persistently reflected in magazines, movies and television, however had been in sharp contrast to the growing evidence that the average women has become heavier over the past decades (Garfinkel and Garner, 1982). Weight control has become synonymous for discipline, personal strength, willpower and success. The unsolvable conflict between cultural demands and biological forces is reflected in the increased pervasiveness of dieting among women (Garner et al., 1980). Accordingly eating disorders can be viewed as contemporary socio-cultural phenomena or so called 'metaphors for our time' (Orbach, 1986). Throughout times women have experienced that social acceptance and approval are directly related to physical appearance; looking attractive is an essential criterion of value for women (Wooley & Wooley, 1985). The association of thinness with desirable social status is considered one of the most significant predisposing factors to the expression of eating disorders, especially affecting vulnerable adolescents who have come to believe that weight control is synonymous with self-esteem and self-control (Bruch, 1978).

THINNESS AS A SYMBOL OF SOCIAL AND SEXUAL FREEDOM

In the early 1960s the image of a slim, long legged and small breasted body shape was promoted by appearance of a female model named the 'Shrimp', who broke with the contemporary voluptuous images of women (Orbach, 1986). However the ideal of thinness came to represent other aspects of socio-cultural change as well. It could be understood as a rejection of the constraints inherent to social class and sex, an attempt to transcend barriers between class, age and sex. Bennett & Gurin (1982) have suggested that the shift from the 'maternal figure', retaining body fat, towards the thin body standard symbolises the expression of female sexual liberation in which slimness has been opposed to fertility: 'the central expression of the new liberated women was her thin body, which came to symbolise athleticism, nonreproductive sexuality and a kind of androgynous independence'. In a study of Beck et al. (1976) the association between the preference for a thinner body shape and a less traditional feminine sex-role affiliation has been

supported. Beck and his colleagues found that women who pre-
ferred a smaller overall shape were less traditionally feminine.

SUCCESSFUL FEMININITY: THE EXCLUSION OF 'MASCULINE' VIRTUES

For young women, developing femininity successfully requires the
assimilation of three essential demands: deference to other people,
converting one's own needs to those of others and seeking self
definition through affiliation (Orbach, 1986). Girls have been traditionally taught that fulfilling other people's needs is more important
than rewarding their own desires. They have been encouraged to
deny and suppress their own inner needs and, as a consequence,
have not been able to develop an authentic sense of entitlement for
their desires. Hence they will not be able to experience themselves
as people with entitled wants, feelings and needs. Anorexia nervosa
has been understood as an exaggerated form of denial as a cultural
value for women while at the same time as a protest against this
cultural rule that constrain a woman's life (Orbach, 1986). The
unfamiliarity with one's own inner sensations, as well as the preoccupation with other people's needs, results in a sense of self that has
become dependent upon the approval of those to whom they must
defer. The self esteem of anorexic patients has appeared to be
extremely dependent upon interpersonal approval and social recognition (Bruch, 1974).

Boskind-Lodahl (1976) found clinical evidence to contend that
women with eating disorders have internalised the cultural standards
of successful femininity in a desperate attempt to avoid social
rejection. Data to support the postulation that anorexic women have
adopted a cultural standard of femininity were found in our recent
study (Weeda-Mannak & Arondeus, 1990). Anorectic women had
lower self esteem than non-eating disordered female controls and the
lack of self esteem was associated with greater femininity. This finding
may not be surprising since, according to Bardwick (1971), women
from an early age tend to be rewarded socially for affiliation, resulting
in their self esteem being strongly tied to interpersonal approval.

The ideal of femininity usually excluded the adoption of so
called 'masculine' virtues such as independence, effectiveness and
the expression of anger and aggression (Wooley & Wooley, 1985).
Women with anorexia nervosa have been found to particularly
shape their life in the cultural expectations of femininity and to
have failed to adopt traditionally masculine attributes (Sitnick &

Katz, 1984; Weeda-Mannak et al., 1990). When compared to a matched control group of non-eating disordered women anorectic and bulimic women were found to score significantly higher on femininity while scoring significantly lower on masculinity. Feministic theorists have identified the socio-cultural environment as an important transmitter of an inferior psychology of women, contributing to the development of eating disorders in particular and mental disorder in women in general.

CONTRADICTORY ROLE DEFINITIONS FOR WOMEN

It was Selvini-Palazzoli (1974) who linked the expression of anorexia nervosa to the new, often contradictory roles for women in modern society. She emphasised that the cultural and social changes such as the admission of women into traditional male preserves such as education and professional careers while previously confined to the role of housewife and mother, tend to aggravate the inner conflicts of women.

'Today, in fact, women are expected to be beautiful, smart and well groomed, and to devote a great deal of time to their personal appearance even while competing in business and the professions. They must have a career and yet be romantic, tender and sweet and in marriage play the part of the ideal wife cum mistress and cum mother who puts away her hard earned diplomas to wash nappies and perform other menial chores' (p. 35).

The changing female sex-role definitions have implied that women are not only supposed to adopt traditional feminine traits but traditional masculine characteristics too. In this respect becoming a female adult might be more difficult than becoming a male adult. According to Selvini-Palazzoli (1974) it is quite obvious that the social pressure to satisfy so many contradictory demands has considerably contributed to unsolvable conflicts in women; especially in those who have adopted a traditional feminine identity, while at the same time incorporating more modern standards for vocational achievement. Also Bardwick (1971) has stressed that women are not only expected to achieve highly in a competitive vocational world, but also to excel in traditional feminine roles. For many women overwhelmed by the fear of losing control in the face of such demands, weight control represents control in other ways of personal functioning.

It has been found in a number of research studies that women with eating disorders display a more than average drive for achievement (Garner et al., 1983; Weeda-Mannak et al., 1983). Women with an increased drive to achieve will enter traditionally male preserves such as higher education and vocational careers. These competitive environments usually demand the adoption of traditional masculine traits such as competitiveness, aggression and initiative. The feminine sex-typed traits that have been reinforced since childhood are quite different from those required masculine attributes needed for a successful vocational career. Within this context a women may fail because she is lacking those masculine attributes or she may succeed but feel guilty about succeeding. Because of the link between the changing body shape at puberty and the intensified conflicting of role expectations for women their body has become the focal point to cope with conflicting achievement and psychosocial demands (Bardwick, 1971).

CONCLUSIONS
The clinical as well as epidemiological finding that eating disorders are overrepresented in women have been held as the most convincing support for the view that socio-cultural factors contribute to the expression of anorexia and bulimia nervosa (Herzog & Copeland, 1985; Szmukler, 1985; Wolf, 1990). In this chapter the importance of female sex-role identity, within the context of other biological and psychological factors which are believed to play a role in the pathogenesis of eating disorders, has been highlighted. Since not all women are suffering from an eating disorder it would be naïve to assume that cultural factors alone can 'cause' the development of anorexia or bulimia nervosa. However there is a widespread belief, particularly among feminist contributors, that there is a continuity in all women's experience which makes them vulnerable for the manifestation of anorexia or bulimia nervosa (Orbach, 1986; Wooley & Wooley, 1985). In this respect it is important to stress the significance of the social- cultural environment in transmitting a psychology for women which tends to deny their biological characteristics, their rights and their needs and makes them believe that denial of selfhood is a symbol of self-worth and autonomy.

REFERENCES
Bardwick J. (1971) *Psychology of women: A study of bio-cultural conflicts.* New York: Harper and Row.
Beck S.B., Ward-Hull C.I., McLear P.M. (1976) Variables related to

women's somatic preferences of the male and female body. *Journal of Personality and Social Psychology*, 34: 1200–1210.

Bennett W.B. & Gurin J. (1982) *The dieter's dilemma: Eating less and weighing more*. New York: Basis Books.

Boskind-Lodahl M. (1976) Cinderella's step-sisters: A feminist perspective on anorexia nervosa and bulimia. *Signs: Journal of Women in Culture and Society*, 2: 342–256.

Bruch H. (1973) *Eating Disorders*. New York, Basic Books.

Bruch H. (1978) *The Golden Cage*. Cambridge: Harvard University Press.

Garfinkel P.E., Garner D.M. (1982) *Anorexia nervosa: A multidimensional perspective*. New York, Bruner Mazel.

Garner D.M., Garfinkel P.E., Schwarz D., Thompson M. (1980) Cultural expectations of thinness in women. *Psychological Reports*, 47: 483–491.

Garner D.M., Olmsted M.P., Polivy J., Garfinkel P.E. (1983) Does anorexia nervosa occur on a continuum? Subgroups of weight-preoccupied women and their relationship to anorexia nervosa. *International Journal of Eating Disorders*, 2: 11–20.

Herzog D.B. & Copeland P.M. (1985) Eating disorders. *New England Journal of Medicine*, 5: 295–303.

Orbach S. (1986) *Hunger strike. The anorectic's struggle as a metaphor for our age*. New York/London: Norton & Company.

Ryle J.A. (1939) Discussion on anorexia nervosa. *Proceedings of Royal Society Medicine*, 32: 735–737.

Selvini-Palazolli M.P. (1974) *Self-starvation. From the intra-psychic to the transpersonal approach to anorexia nervosa*. London: Chaucer Publishing Co.

Sitnick T. & Katz J.L. (1984) Sex role identity and anorexia nervosa. *International Journal of Eating Disorders*, 3: 81–89.

Szmukler G.I. (1985) The epidemiology of anorexia nervosa and bulimia. *Journal of Psychiatric Research*, 19: 143-153.

Weeda-Mannak W.L., Drop M.J., Smits F., Strijbosch L.W. & Bremer J.J. (1983) Toward an early recognition of anorexia nervosa. *International Journal of Eating Disorders*, 2: 27–37.

Weeda-Mannak W.L., Arondeus J.M. & Takens R.J. (1990) Sex-role identity and anorexia nervosa. In: Drenth J.D., Sergeant J.A. and Takens R.J. (Eds). *European perspectives in psychology*. Vol 2. Chicester: Wiley & Sons.

Wolf N. (1990) *The Beauty Myth*. London, Chatto & Windus.

Wooley S.C. & Wooley O.W. (1985) Intensive outpatient and residential treatment for bulimia. In: Garner D.M. & Garfinkel P.E. (Eds). *Handbook of psychotherapy for anorexia nervosa and bulimia*. New York/London: Guilford Press.

CHAPTER 3

On the
Relationship between Daughters
and Mothers with Regard to
Bulimia Nervosa
Karin Bell

The life-history of a bulimic woman is traced up to the
outbreak of her symptoms. Several aspects of female
development which promote the beginnings of a bulimia
syndrome are expounded with the help of this case
example. The ultimate triggering of the syndrome is the
adolescent problem of dissolution of emotional ties,
which the patient is unable to cope with due to earlier
shortcomings in her strivings towards autonomy. In
detail, this means excessive stimulation in the early
mother-daughter relationship which renders it impossible for the infant to withdraw. The daughter cannot
cope appropriately with the rapprochement phase, since
she identifies with a dependent mother who reacts
anxiously towards her daughter's independence. The
daughter develops the same ego ideal as her mother,
that of a 'mother who is only good'. Certain specifically
female caring attitudes and aggressive inhibitions are
'inherited' as a result. All in all, the family atmosphere
is chaotic and offers little security, with no clear boundaries between the generations and with the 'parentising'
of the children. The girl is given no affirmation of her
female sexuality, while the father, often an alcoholic,
tries to seduce her into dependence on him. Changes
in cultural expectations are also mentioned: the self-

sacrificing woman was the ideal of Western societies up to the end of the '60s. The growing demand for female independence after that intensifies the specifically female conflict between loyalty to a relationship and autonomy.

MARTHA

Martha is 17 years old. Enrolled for therapy by her mother, she is also brought to therapy by her mother. Both mother and daughter leave it up to me at first to decide whether I want to see them together or separately. Martha cannot make up her mind when asked what she would like, so that we stand wavering in the hall for a while. In the end the mother decides: 'I'll go, so that you can relate your worries undisturbed for once.'

In 1980, in the 3rd edition of the Diagnostic and Statistical Manual of Mental Disorders (DSM III), bulimia nervosa was defined as a syndrome in its own right and differentiated from anorexia nervosa. The symptom of morbid hunger attacks with or without subsequent self-induced vomiting has, admittedly, already been described within the context of other illnesses: however, the bulimia syndrome has only emerged in the stricter sense of a differentiated new form of eating disorder since the '60s and '70s. A sudden rise in the number of patients in the '80s would seem to suggest an epidemic. This 'epidemic' probably began in the late '40s. The breeding-ground: a post-war affluent society in which success, performance and food played a large part and were interlinked in many different ways. As bulimia nervosa is a sex-linked illness – 95% of sufferers are women – it is natural to seek culturally-linked causes of the illness in the changing conceptions of the female sex as described, for example, by Schmauch (1987) for the Federal Republic of Germany. After the war sexual division of labour was re-established in a relatively rigid form: 'Mothers were almost always there, like a natural and inevitable unity of love and control, or they were absent, and the separation meant guilt and distress' (Schmauch, 1987, p.39). Tension arose between the ideal of mother and housewife and the wish or necessity for a career of one's own, frequently described as 'making money on the side', which conveyed itself to the daughters as a message to be both like their mothers and to become their opposites. More possibilities seem to present themselves to women from around 1970 onwards. Unfortunately, this new freedom very quickly turned into demands made upon women by society 'the professed conception of modern women requires that she is capable of integrating incompatible restraints and interests, fully in command of the situation' (Schmauch, loc. cit. p.40). Mitscherlich-Nielsen (1978) outlines the situation as follows: 'Role expectations in society are beginning to flounder more and more ... conflicting demands are beginning to make themselves felt: women are supposed to learn to make themselves independent in our culture, while at the same time they are unable to exploit any opportunities of freedom, since the necessary family, professional and psychological conditions required for this are lacking.'

'This makes them feel quite worthless. They are supposed to be empathic mothers, fully understanding the complicated psychological problems of their children, make good house-wives and, what is more, be equal partners to their husbands, also capable of asserting themselves professionally. These are demands hardly anyone can meet.' (p.688)

Habermas (1990) is also of the opinion that one of the historical pre-conditions for bulimia is to be found in the changing roles of the sexes. So long as women define themselves essentially through and in their relationship with the male sex, their independence remains such in appearance only. The relatively new, seemingly contradictory, expectation put on young women to be independent for the other sex (ie most important, it would seem, is that they appear to be independent), which becomes more apparent when analysing advertising than in social-psychological studies, fits in with the physical ideal that slimness equates to attractiveness for others and autonomy. '... new, at least regarding it's universal propagation in Western society, ... is the clear association of a slim body and the autonomy it symbolises with the ideal of sexual attractiveness, which threatens to betray that autonomy' (Habermas, 1990, p.205).

The finding of one's own identity and the dissolution of emotional ties with the primary family are adolescent tasks in the maturation process which occupy the typical bulimic woman during the beginnings of the symptom complex. The following chapter will discuss those patients whose symptom complex first appears within the framework of adolescent conflicts in the process of gaining emotional freedom. I shall not refer to patients who develop bulimic symptoms in the course of other neurotic illnesses, nor to those patients with a borderline personality structure.

Martha has suffered from morbid hunger attacks for two years. These seldom result in self-induced vomiting, so that, she has put on about 5 kg. She is not very overweight though, as she is basically tall and stately, and is rather plump at most. When she was only 10 or 11 years old she did think that she was too fat, although she was slim then. She went on a starvation diet for a while but never became as slim as she had wanted to. Two years ago she had to break off a stay abroad prematurely. Since her return she has been suffering from binge eating attacks several times a week, when she has to keep on eating until she 'has the feeling that she will burst'. She then gives a typical account: repeated attempts to lose weight through rigorous dieting, fear of losing control in a morbid hunger attack, while at the same time thoughts of food occupy her mind as soon as she has some peace and quiet.

With the help of Martha's life-history, I shall attempt to trace certain stages of development and highlight factors which could promote the beginnings of bulimia. At the same time I shall mention certain development crises specific to womanhood.

DEVELOPMENT INTO WOMANHOOD BEGINS WITH SEX DETERMINATION AT BIRTH
On the one hand this view, held in particular by Stoller and Kleeman, stresses the influence of cognitive maturation processes on development sexual identity. Sex determination at birth initiates a socialisation process which teaches the girl that she is feminine, as well as how and in what areas a female family member (and the part of society her family represents) should act (Kleeman, 1977). On the other hand, prime importance is attached to environmental influences (Stoller, 1977)

When the girl begins to feel like a girl on the basis of sex determination imparted to her through her environment, she models herself on her mother. Her aim then is to apply this model, to examine it and to develop herself in her own way. This separation from the mother and its flexible implementation is a difficult task in adolescence. The outcome is frequently obdurate separation: 'I am not at all like my mother', or an identity diffusion, whereby differences between mother and daughter are hardly noticed: 'We are like two sisters.' Martha's model is a woman who only feels satisfied when she has a baby to look after. Martha was born when her older sister reached the age of puberty. She was the youngest child, but only because her father denied her mother the wish to have more children. Now that Martha has finally picked up the courage to begin therapy, there is another baby in the family: Her mother is looking after her sister's child. Although this baby is only six months old, her sister is already planning a second child 'so that everything doesn't centre around the baby'. One has the impression that the family needs the external reality of a second baby in order to keep the baby at a suitable distance.

When Martha was 3 years old her father was made unemployed. Her mother looked for a job, which was first experienced as guilty and painful separation, but later continued, although the external necessity no longer existed. A certain ambivalent attitude on the side of Martha's mother became apparent here with regard to her feminine self-definition: to be a woman means to be a mother.

Results of infant observation in the past few years have changed our conception of infant capabilities and demonstrated subtleties in the co-ordination of the relationship between mother and child hitherto unknown. Although it is true that Winnicott (1974), with his differentiation between the 'holding mother' and object mother, has already demonstrated two different maternal offerings of relationship which correspond to the various relationship desires in infants in various 'states'. Brazelton (1983) stresses the significance of rhythmic sequences in the relationship between mother and child, whereby states of withdrawal and receptiveness to stimuli must alternate. Martha describes most impressively the unrest and hectic pace at home which arises because the baby is experienced as someone to whom one has to devote a great deal of one's time. The result is probably a chaotic over- stimulation, which means that peaceful phases of privacy and inward contemplation cannot be experienced. This could depict a basal prerequisite for obsessive and impulsive behaviour.

THE RAPPROCHEMENT PHASE AS A CRITICAL PERIOD IN FEMALE
DEVELOPMENT OF IDENTITY

Girls begin to describe themselves as girls at the age of 15 months:
an identification process with female characteristics now begins,
for which the mother serves as a model. At the same time in the
rapprochement phase development of an identity separate from
that of the mother begins to take place. Chodorow (1974) accentu-
ates the significance of the relationship for female identity development, which results from the fact that separation from the mother
is not necessary for the development of female identity. I consider
it a specifically female task to find a sphere appropriate to one's
own needs for the relationship to the mother and separation from
her. As independence is a culturally positively rated term at the
moment, yet women cannot follow culturally pre-set standards
here as they are not intended for women in this form. Woman's
independence, after all, is supposed to provide a function in the
relationship which takes the load off and at the same time attracts
the man.

During the rapprochement phase certain forms of toilet training
can arouse doubts in the child as to whether it has command of its
own body or whether the body belongs to the mother. This feeling
is intensified through budding, possibly forbidden, masturbation
around this time. Thus proneness to disturbances abounds. There
are mothers who reject in this phase and mothers who monopolize.
Whatever the case, it is a turbulent period, demanding a great deal
of stamina in self-confidence from mothers, for they are, in quick
succession, both the object of clinging affection and the object of
rejection. As the mother relives her relationship toward her own
mother in her relationship with her daughter, she also relives her
own painful separation and individualisation. That puts a strain on
her as the mother relives again the 'loss of her own mother and the
loss of her baby' (Bergmann, 1982).

Martha cannot recount anything from this period. She was
considered to be a well-behaved, rather anxious child who had
problems coping with the separation of going to kindergarten.
Toilet training was unproblematic, and there were no stubborn
phases. It is precisely the inconspicuousness of this phase which
would seem to us to be an indication of a possible disturbance.
Martha's mother is anxious when the children leave the house

and always wants to know where they are. In addition, she 'does not appear to be able to live without a baby'. Thus it is unlikely that she could understand Martha's wish to 'move away' from her. It seems that Martha has adapted herself to the anxieties of her mother, who could not endure separation.

A further indication of the difficulties Martha's mother has with separation and individualisation is that she returned to her own mother's house shortly after her marriage and has lived closely together with her mother ever since. What is more, she dissipates her energies on various external demands, and can hardly bring her own plans to an end. It is thus doubtful whether Martha's mother experienced 'the loss of her baby and the loss of her mother' in the rapprochement phase. On the contrary, her behaviour would make it seem that she is continually trying to avert experiences of separation and loss. Thus Martha cannot develop any aggression in her gaining of independence. Instead, when she sees how her mother is worn out by the demands of others, but at the same time repeatedly offers to spoil them, she will experience an inner conflict as to what she wants from her mother. On the one hand, she isn't supposed to become independent, while on the other hand she no longer wishes to burden her mother. This dilemma frequently crops up as a transference/counter-transference constellation in therapy sessions with bulimic patients: the passive demanding attitude results in the therapist unthinkingly becoming more active. This caring attention does not satisfy the patient, however. Behind the passivity lies a claim to independence.

In Martha's family the climate is also such that differences and separation are to a large extent dispensed with. External and internal boundaries merge into one. On the one hand, the family has no outward private life, the door is always open, while on the other hand there is no inner private life: friends, clothes, personal feelings, and sexual experiences are shared by the women in the family, with the father the only outsider. And so the contours between mother and daughter, already more difficult to define because they are the same sex, become blurred.

THOSE INHERENT TENDENCIES IN THE GIRL WHICH LEAD TO
SEPARATION INDIVIDUALISATION PROBLEMS ARE INTENSIFIED BY AN
EGO-IDEAL WHICH UPHOLDS THE CONCEPTION OF AN 'IDEAL MOTHER'

According to Jacobson (1978), ego-identifications with realistic parental images arise in girls when the aims and attainment norms of the parents are adopted. The girl then identifies herself in particular with the mother. Unavoidable or avoidable frustration through the mother leads to primitive ideal images of the self and the love objects turning into a unified ego-ideal, which ties on to the grandiose desires of the preoedipal child and its belief in parental omnipotence. Thus a sacrificing and caring ideal is formed in women, in which any experience of separation- individualisation or realisation of their own interests following a phase of intensive mothering (eg., when a brother or sister is born or the mother goes out to work), contribute to the formation of this ideal if the familiar climate offers no possibility for dealing with the disappointment it arouses in the child.

In Martha's case the mother went back to work when she was three years old. Martha's mother is the eldest of a family of six. She felt forced to take over responsibility for her younger brothers and sisters at an early age, as her mother suffered from depressive moods and her father died when she was 15 years old. She was thus forced into early independence which, however, instead of furthering her own strivings towards autonomy, became independence 'for others'.

Martha's mother is to a great extent committed to an excessive, motherly ego-ideal, including its negative individuation in favour of caring for others: she cannot handle disappointment and rage, which she does not experience as necessary developmental steps, but as a questioning of her motherly capabilities, with the result that she passes on her own aggressive inhibitions to her daughter.

THE OEDIPAL PHASE CAN ONLY BE ADEQUATELY OVERCOME IF THERE IS
SUFFICIENT SEPARATION FROM THE MOTHER

While attention has hitherto been directed to the relationship between Martha and her mother, I shall now describe her relationship with her brother and her father, which presents itself like a negative of the afore-mentioned relationship between the two women. While the women have a 'really good' relationship, the men are more or less left out in the cold. The father is consciously left out of things, the brother keeps himself out of things. In Martha's eyes her father, and his drinking in particular, is to blame for her mother's unhappiness. Usually rather quiet and withdrawn, he becomes loud when he has been drinking and reproaches her mother. Martha thinks everything would be okay if the father didn't drink, and in a way she is right, if the father in his fondness for drink is interpreted as a symbol of the inadequate attempts of the whole family to free themselves of emotional ties.

Father and daughter had a very close relationship until puberty set in. They used to exchange a lot of affection, which Martha sensed her father didn't get enough of from her mother. Since reaching the age of puberty, Martha has been on her mother's side and avoids any physical contact with her father.

Incestuous anxieties reactivated through puberty suggest themselves here as the cause of estrangement between father and daughter. Martha is probably afraid to steer her father's seductive overtures, owing to her lack of separation individuation abilities. She was particularly offended, however, by disparaging remarks from her father about her body in adolescence. Emphasis has often been put on the importance of the father for the development of positive female sexuality, but the mother can also play a positively strengthening role if she encourages her daughter towards development into a sexually perceptive woman. However, Martha's mother seems to have given up as far as her own sexual attractiveness is concerned: she also thinks of herself as too fat, ie, unattractive, and has retreated into the role of the caring mother.

The 30 year old brother – thin, like his father – still lives in the primary family as well. There is an incestuous touch to her relationship with him, with frequent exchanges of physical affection. One would think Martha was in love with him when she speaks of him. The brother, however, also appears to be a substitute husband for the mother in the sense of the blurred borderlines between the generations in this family.

Although her brother's acknowledgement of her femininity is important for and beneficial to Martha's female identity, the close relationship between the two (who differ greatly in age) seems like an attempt to reconcile desires appropriate to their age for a heterosexual relationship, ie., strivings towards dissolution of emotional ties with the primary family and the desire to bind to the family. A trans-generational passing on of unsolved autonomy conflicts is thus to be found on both the female and the male side.

With the women in the family, these show themselves in eating disorders and/or depression: Martha's grandmother was overweight – she now has diabetes mellitus – and suffered from depression as well. Martha's mother has weight problems, and there are signs of neurotic depression (inner unrest, state of exhaustion), Martha herself has bulimia. The three women are both united and divided through cooking and eating. The grandmother is envious of the others since she has had to stick to a diet. Although the mother considers herself too fat, she cannot summon up the energy to go on a diet and her cooking is rich in calories. Martha has been trying to lose weight since she reached puberty and would like most of all 'her and her mother to lose weight together.' Working from the basis of similar inner conflicts in the three women, the obvious question would seem to be why Martha has fallen ill with bulimia, of all things. Recognition of bulimia as an illness has undoubtedly played a part in this, providing Martha with a frame for a compromisable solution to her conflicts. Further external factors are the increasing affluence of a family which was still poor in the grandmother's and in the mother's day and a greater demand for self-control of oral impulses, compared to the days when 'the way to a man's heart was through his stomach'.

On the male side, increased alcohol consumption and/or uncontrolled impulsiveness are to be found.

Eating disorders have two-sided beginnings. Possible causes of the disorder, and how they can occur in early childhood have hitherto been described. The changes which occurred in puberty have already been portrayed in Martha's relationship with her father.

The sex-linked separation-individuation conflicts between mother and daughter normally flare up again in puberty 'until they can leave each other alone'. Not with Martha, however: when puberty begins to set in she has a brief anorexic phase, like those not uncommonly found in young girls. At the same time, however, Martha begins to identify completely with the cares and troubles of her mother. She is upset and sad that her mother 'lets people exploit her to the full'. Whenever the tries to assert herself aggres-sively against her mother, she feels guilty and as bad as the father she runs down. Instead of the forthcoming emotional freedom, an intensified bond results in which Martha seems to sense vaguely that something isn't quite right. And so when she was 15 years old she decided to live abroad for a while 'to get away from home for once'. Having resolved not to let herself be spoilt any more, she rejected the possibly excessively caring nature of her guest family in an extremely undiplomatic manner, which led to conflicts with them: an attempt at emotional freedom with the wrong object. The bulimic symptoms have been there since her return. Habermas (1990) describes the family background of the bulimic patient as offering little security, and burdened with a great deal of open conflicts. Thus the patient prematurely takes on an adult role in early adolescence, a well as responsibility for other members of the family. Greater efforts have to be made to ward off regressive desires, and independence has to be secured by way of rigid self-control. Satisfaction of regressive needs ensues by way of altruistic withdrawal (A. Freud, 1936).

The patients pay a high price for this since their desire 'to be there for others' is maintained by unconscious motives which serve to ward off separation anxieties, conflicting strivings must be kept from being perceived. This leads to aggressive strivings, even harm-less ones such as the desire for a room of one's own, only being perceived as vague and confused inner tension, not able to be named. The bulimic patient tries to dispel this inner tension in a binge eating attack and in doing so threatens anew her modest self-image. The symbolic function of eating is frequently referred to, whereby the binge eating is portrayed as an unsuccessful attempt to embody the mother, only to eject her in the subsequent vomiting. This moving towards and moving away from the mother in the rapprochement phase was thus repeated regressively on an oral level. Martha's life history and that of other bulimic women does not rule out an interpretation of this kind. Along with the symbolic significance, however, eating would also appear to be an aid to removing inner tension and feelings of emptiness which occur in these women because they have never experienced their inner sphere as something separate from the mother. Perception of their libidinal and aggressive strings is therefore greatly lacking, and so they cannot search for possible solutions.

Most women, however, are familiar with the conflicts which subject bulimic patients to failure. The conflict between the loyalty which regulates a relationship and legitimate separation aggression is intensified by changing cultural expectations and ideals. Many women know the ego-ideal of a mother who is only good, who sacrifices her own desires. They more or less cope with the rapprochement phase, whereby identification with the 'separation' side of the mother, which would make their own autonomy easier, seldom occurs.

I conclude my thoughts with perhaps a rather individual interpretation of the tale of 'Rumpelstiltskin'. In Rumpelstiltskin, I see in the king's daughter (who was not acknowledged because she was not named) that wild, aggressively demanding part of her self. It is not until she succeeds in integrating this part of her, and only when she can stop fulfilling father's (and mother's) ridiculous wish to spin gold out of straw, that she can become creative and fruitful.

REFERENCES

Bergmann, A. (1982) Considerations about the Development of the Girl during Separation-Individuation Process in Mendell, D. (Ed) *Early Female Development*. Lancaster: MPT

Brazelton, B.T. (1983) Precursors for the Development of Emotions in Early Infancy. In R. Plutchik & H. Kellerman (Eds.) *Emotion: Theory, Research and Experience, Vol.2: Emotions in Early Development*. New York: Academic Press

Chodorow, N. (1974) Family Structure and Feminine Personality. In Rosaldo, MZ., Lamphere, L. (Eds) *Women, Culture and Society*. Stanford: University Press

Freud, A. (1936) *Das Ich und die Abwehrmechanismen*. München: Kindler

Habermas, T. (1990) *Heißhunger*. Frankfurt: Fischer

Jacobson, E. (1978) *Das Selbst und die Welt der Objekte*. Frankfurt: Suhrkamp

Kleeman, J.A. (1977) Freud's Views on Early Female Sexuality in the Light of Direct Child Observation. Blum, H.P.(Ed) *Female Psychology*. N.York: IUP

Mitscherlich-Nielsen, M. (1978) *Zur Psychoanalyse der Weiblichkeit*. Psyche 32, p.669–694

Schmauch, U. (1987) *Anatomie und Schicksal*. Frankfurt: Fischer

Stoller, R.S. (1977) Primary Femininity in Blum, H.P. (Ed) *Female Psychology*. New York: IUP

Winnicot, D.W. (1974) *Reifungsprozesse und fördernde Umwelt*. Stuttgart: Klett

CHAPTER 4

How Important is Body Image for Normal Weight Bulimics? Implications for Research and Treatment

Judith Bullerwell-Ravar

Fear of becoming obese, feelings of dissatisfaction and disgust towards one's own body and desperate attempts to control weight have long been considered 'proof' of a disordered attitude towards body image in women with eating disorders. However the comparison of women with bulimia and women with no current eating problems in France throws a new light upon this belief. This chapter examines more closely the utility of the concept of 'body image distortion' and asks if clinicians should continue to isolate and 'treat' the implied aberration.

BODY DISSATISFACTION AND THE BULIMIC SYNDROME

Body dissatisfaction, like self-disparagement and body image distortion, is considered to be an important factor in the psychopathology of the bulimic syndrome. Fear of fat and desperate attempts to lose weight are often quoted as proof of a body image that is as pathological as the eating disorder itself.

The links between body image and disordered eating have been demonstrated by a substantial amount of research, including comparative studies on size estimation, attitudes towards the body including dissatisfaction, fear of obesity, need to control or lose weight. (Slade, 1985; Slade, 1990)

In France the urgent request of bulimic patients – whatever their weight – when they first consult a clinician in order to stop their binge eating behaviour, is firstly not to gain weight, and secondly to lose some.

The Catch 22 aspect of the relationship between the fear of obesity and binge eating has been abundantly demonstrated. The bulimic panics at the fantasy of an 'Alice in Wonderland' body which threatens to expand in an unlimited way unless control is exerted over it relentlessly, and permanently. The paradox is that the dieting and restricting behaviour tend lead to the very effects that the patient does not wish, since excessive restraint tends to trigger binge eating.

The sociocultural model of desirable slenderness can also complicate the nutritional problem. To correspond to this model, a woman often has to weigh less than her normal biological weight. In bulimic women insistence on such a goal reinforces both dieting and binge eating behaviour. The honest clinician who points out in the first session that in order to eliminate the binge eating it will probably be necessary to accept to weigh 1 or 2 kilos above the presenting ideal is likely to never see the horrified patient again!

For all the above reasons, and whatever the theoretical background of the therapist, the bulimic patient's body image is considered 'disordered' since although her weight is often normal in medical terms, she panics at the idea of becoming fat. Proof of a more objective body image is usually considered to be the acceptance by the patient of her current weight, and a less obsessive desire to lose the necessary number of pounds to reach her 'ideal' weight.

Therapists, faced with a bulimic patient, often adopt a treatment package, which includes food and mood monitoring, nutritional education and cognitive-behavioural methods, as well as insight-directed therapy. Certain clinicians have wondered however, given the importance of body image for the patient, if success would not be more rapid if the accent were placed initially on the pathological aspects of body image, especially as most research shows that bulimics, once cured, are satisfied with their body image.

PROBLEMS OF RESEARCH AND TREATMENT CONCERNING BODY IMAGE DISTORTION

The problems are threefold, and concern:

- the concept itself. What exactly do we mean by body image?
- the measurement of body image. What exactly are we measuring?
- evaluation techniques, both in research and treatment.

THE CONCEPT OF BODY IMAGE

The practical definition of body image used in this paper is the physical and cognitive representation of the body which underlies and includes attitudes of acceptance and rejection, this is however at best a working definition. For what body, and what body image are we talking about? The psychodynamic definitions, which emphasize the symbolic and fantasy aspects of body image, cannot be tested in a scientific research model. Other definitions, depending on the background of the researcher, may privilege the physical perception of the body and or parts of it, or on the other hand insist on subjective attitudes of acceptance and rejection. Other aspects include physiological, biological, social, psychological and cultural elements.

But it has been demonstrated that body image can be modified over time and that its limits are not fixed. Clothes can extend the image, a hat for example, or even an object held in the hand. (Schilder, 1950; Fisher, 1986). So we are dealing with a complex concept, lacking well-defined contours, not only for bulimic patients, but also for clincans and researchers!

Thus Fisher (1986) includes in his scholarly review of research on body image, for lack of a precise scientific definition, any study which deals with 'how individuals view and assign meaning to their own body' (p.1)

MEASUREMENT OF BODY IMAGE

Researchers into the body image of bulimics have tried to study this concept in two ways, by physical measurement or by cognitive attitude. In the first case, the subject is asked to reproduce either her whole silhouette or parts of her body by means of an apparatus, more or less sophisticated, in order to measure the difference between the objective size and those indicated by the subject. Too big a difference is supposed to correspond to an erroneous evaluation on the subject's part, corresponding to body image distortion.

However, the connection has not been proved, especially as it has been shown in other research that non-bulimics and controls overestimate their size as much as bulimics. The body image problem of bulimic patients is therefore concerned with more than erroneous perception of the body.

The second type of measurement concerns the attitude towards the body, linked to the cognitive representation of what is positive or negative in the body, often measured by questionnaires.

Results of body image attitude and dissatisfaction scales are more discriminating than physical measurements. If all women wish to lose a few kilos, attitudes of anxiety and body rejection are more specifically bulimic. So this type of measure does enable us to distinguish between bulimic women and the others. However in this dichotomous distinction the connection with weight, which has its part in both types of measurement, is not very clear. However, weight is obviously an important element in how a woman perceives and feels about her body. Moreover, weight dissatisfaction has been shown to be generalised among women in industrialised countries among the female population, not only bulimics and anorexics (e.g. Rodin, Silberstein & Striegel-Moore, 1985; Birtchnell, Dolan & Lacey, 1987).

Research findings also disagree on whether bulimics and anorexics really overestimate their body size more than controls in size-estimation techniques. As to the question whether body image distortion – and indeed body image – is stable over time or not, the case in favour of stability put forward by Garfinkel et al, (1978) was generally accepted until quite recently.

Faced with these results researchers have tried both to explain the contradictory findings, and refine measurement techniques. One of the paths followed was to distinguish between cognitive elements (induced by questions such as 'what do you *think* your size really is?' and emotional, subjective feelings (induced by questions such as 'what do you *feel* your size is?'). Slade (1985) first suggested that different aspects of the body image were being tapped by the different techniques used and hypothesised on the one hand a relatively stable cognitive attitude to the body size and on the other a perceptual aspect that is more influenced by external factors and the emotional state of the subject.

More recently however, he has come to believe that the body image of bulimics and anorexics is 'uncertain and unstable' rather than 'distorted' (Slade, 1990). This position corresponds to recent research findings (Norris, 1984; Collins et al., 1987; Brinded et al.,

1990). For example Norris found that bulimics and anorexics changed their judgement about their body after mirror confrontation, whereas controls did not.

Our own research, based on in-depth interviews, is that, even though perception of body size may not be stable, the *attitude* to the body usually is, especially when this attitude is negative, as in the case of bulimic and anorexic patients. However body image attitude corresponds to a continuum, which does not exactly reproduce that of eating disorders. It is not because a woman is unhappy with her body that she becomes bulimic.

Certain bulimics, who consider that vomiting has provided a solution to their weight problem, make a distinction between the body such as it appears on the outside, to other people, and which is satisfying provided is it controlled by vomiting, and the body perceived from the inside, which is fantasised as potentially obese.

EVALUATION

Evaluation of research and therapy of body image runs up against another problem, concerning the difficulty in separating body image from other aspects of self-image, and especially self-esteem.

If cured bulimics have improved self-esteem, self-image and body image, as well as a lesser degree of depression, it is difficult to decide which factor is the most instrumental in the process, since they are linked together. To try to isolate the body image from a more global conception, such as self-image, is an extremely difficult exercise.

SHOULD CLINICIANS 'TREAT' THEIR PATIENT'S BODY IMAGE?

Given this complexity is it possible to treat body image, and if so, how? The following elements need to be taken into consideration:

Firstly, as well as the problems concerning body image already mentioned, the therapist also has to deal with the difficulty of the patient in knowing exactly what is her body image *in the present*.

If we can question Slade's emphasis on an 'unstable' body image, to the extent that control subjects also have a modifiable body image, eating-disordered patients do indeed have an 'uncertain' body image in the present. This uncertainty can moreover be explained. The anguish of bulimics is turned towards the future, where they fear to become obese, and/or towards the past, where they have often been through a period of obesity. When people say that the bulimic is a frustrated anorexic, this comes from the desire to put a maximum gap between the danger of obesity and themselves. This fear is not necessarily unfounded, many bulimics have known a past experience of obesity, which was experienced as traumatising.

More often than not, bulimic women do not live their body in the present and therefore have difficulty in representing their actual body to themselves or describing it to others. They have only a virtual image of their body in the present. It is for this reason that certain bulimics and anorexics cannot say in good faith what is their body image, and indeed need constant reassurance from outside to bolster their virtual image. However these outside indications do not reassure them for very long, and especially not further than the next food intake. They do not avoid the mirror simply because they see themselves as obese, but also because they cannot integrate what they see in it as belonging to them. Weighing scales may play the role of external censor or gauge for some bulimics, other people's scrutiny and remarks for others. However these signs, if positive, only reassure the patient for a short time, not permanently, whilst any negative reinforcement is accepted without question.

Secondly, our own research, using in-depth interviews of three groups (bulimics, ex-bulimics, controls) (see research note at end), indicates that, even though the desire to lose weight is a presenting symptom, this desire is shared *quantitatively* by non-eating-disordered women. The problem is a *qualitative* one, depending on a cognitive set in bulimics, who have a greater fear of obesity and a greater fear of lack of control over food, which will lead to obesity. As a consequence they have a lack of tolerance of any weight exceeding their desired weight – which corresponds not only to 'desirable thinness', but also to a protective blanket against obesity.

Finally, the same research also indicates that the primary problem is not one of body image perception. A sub-group of about 30% of bulimics admitted in the course of their interview that for them the problem was the danger of lack of control rather than a refusal to acknowledge their actual body size. On the other hand, a small percentage of controls had problems with acceptance of their body.

The results of the ex-bulimics tends to indicate that the problem is one of self-acceptance and self-esteem in a larger sense that merely corporal. This result is confirmed by factor analyses of body image tests, in which the eating disorders continuum does not coincide with that of body image dissatisfaction.

The accent placed on improving body image as a means to help bulimics may therefore be less important than originally accepted by clinicians. This could explain the difficulty in separating this aspect of the problem from others such as self-esteem. In France, the body image issue seems to be important on the surface and in the discourse of bulimic patients, but in-depth interviews bring out that this aspect masks more important issues, such as self-confidence and self-esteem and is more an expression of these than the cause of them.

WHICH METHODS CAN BE MOST USEFUL FOR BODY IMAGE
IMPROVEMENTS?

Given this situation, methods which are considered harsh and unpleasant by the patients – such as confrontation with a mirror – may increase their resistance.

When behavioural therapists use methods of 'exposure and response prevention' it is usually in cases where the patient cannot avoid the problem in daily life (e.g. phobias) and he or she has come to therapy in order to solve this specific problem. In the case of the bulimic, the therapeutic request is not to work on the body image, but to lose weight. Thus the 'therapeutic' shock of mirror confrontation is felt to be an aggression by the bulimic patient and a very experienced therapist is needed to deal with this. However, in the case of hospitalisation, the video can be used to show that patient that she has made progress afer a certain time.

A method which enables treatment of body image in a global context is cognitive therapy, since the negative certitudes of the subject are systematically questioned, in order to help her find out what is behind them. Quite often, the bulimic, unable to defend her belief rationally, will herself discover the reason behind it (e.g. fear of failure, fear of not being good enough), thereby reinforcing her

<u>self esteem</u>. The rational demonstration of how the body works and nutritional education can also be useful.

However the treatment of bulimia is a slow process, one of maturation. The body image at the outset is vested with a magic power, that of being able to arrange everything in the bulimic's life, provided that it corresponds to the fixed ideal. It is only when she understands that the eating disorder hides another problem, and accepts to look at what is behind it that she can begin to work on body image, in its relationship to self-image and self-esteem. Only then can she begin to distinguish between the fear of obesity and rejection of her body image, to examine the difficulty of living with her body in the present, and the attitude towards food and the ideal body of her family.

As to the explanation of why body image is so important to bulimics, our research findings lead us to believe that the attitude of the bulimic woman to her body depends on the attitude of her family, especially that of her mother and father, and the importance they attach to norms of slenderness in the family circle, more than on wider cultural norms. We have found that in France that most mothers of bulimics themselves have a problem with food or weight or body image, or all three.

On the other hand, comparison of our results from France with those of Fallon & Rozin (1985) in the USA tend to prove that there are cultural differences insofar as body image is concerned, and that the American female preoccupation with the body is not a universal model in Western industrialised countries.

Food, after all, has a social and cultural meaning, which enables a person to mark his/her assimilation or rejection of a cultural or a collective identity. For the bulimic, like everyone else, the family is a place of social, relational and nutritional apprenticeship. The manipulation of food, body image and relations are thus linked together. In a bulimic family, the mother-daughter relationship often revolves around the daughter's body and eating habits, which become a place of symbolic struggle and manipulation between the two protagonists.

To isolate body image as a therapeutic objective risks to reinforce the patient in her belief that body image is indeed the most important thing in life – especially if the therapist is male . . .

REFERENCES

Birtchnell, S.A., Dolan, B.M. & Lacey, H.J. (1987) Body Size Distortion in Non-eating Disordered Women, *International Journal of Eating Disorders*, 6 (3): 385–391

Brinded, P., Bushnell, J., McKenzie, J. & Wells, J.E. (1990) Body-Image Dostortion Revisited: Temporal Instability of Body Image Distortion in Anorexia Nervosa, *International Journal of Eating Disorders*, 9 (6); 695–701.

Collins, J., Beumont, P. ,Touyz, S., Krass, J., Thompson, P. & Philips, T. (1987) Variability in Body Shape Perception in Anorexic, Bulimic, Obese, and Control Subjects, *International Journal of Eating Disorders*, 6; 633–638

Fallon, A. & Rozin, P. (1985) Sex Differences in Perceptions of Desirable Body Shape, *Journal of Abnormal Psychology*, 94(1): 102–105

Fisher, S. (1986) *Development and Structure of the Body Image*, Laurence Erlbaum Associates, Hillsdale, 2 vols.

Garfinkel, P., Moldofsky, H., Garner, D., Stancer, H. & Coscina, D. (1978) Body Awareness in Anorexia Nervosa; Disturbances in body image and satiety. *Psychosomatic Medicine*, 38: 327–336

Norris, D.L. (1984) The Effects of Mirror Confrontation on Self-Estimation of Body Dimension in Anorexia Nervosa, Bulimia and Two Control Groups, *Psychological Medicine*, 14: 835–842

Rodin, J., Silberstein, L.R. & Striegel-Moore, R.H. (1985) Women and Weight: A Normative Discontent, pp. 267–307 in Sonderegger, T.B. (Ed.): Nebraska *Symposium on Motivation: Vol. 32. Psychology and Gender*, Lincoln, University of Nebraska Press.

Schilder, P. (1950) *The Image and the Appearance of the Human Body*, London, Kegan, Paul, Trench, Trubner.

Slade, P.D. (1985) A Review of Body Image Studies in Anorexia Nervosa and Bulimia Nervosa, *Journal of Psychiatric Research*, 19: 255–265.

Slade, P.D. (1990) Body Image Distortion: A Review of the Literature, *BASH Magazine,* [*July*], 9, 7, pp. 196–197, 222.

RESEARCH NOTE

The author has looked at matched samples of normal-weight bulimics, ex-bulimics and non eating-disordered controls, in order to establish the extent to which attitudes towards body image differed between eating disordered and non eating-disordered French females.

Besides a semi-structured interview on self-image and body-image, the subjects filled in the E.A.T. (40-item version), and three other measures of body image: two scales concerned with body dissatisfaction, the first one dealing with global attitude, the second one with detailed parts of the body, and finally a replica of the Fallon & Rozin drawings research, using a similar protocol by two French researchers, M.Chiva and C.Fischler, called How Fat is Fat?

The interview dealt with weight and family weight histories, as well as attitudes to body image. The results indicated firstly that the desired weight of the bulimic population is close to that of the other groups, and remains within what is considered normal by the medical profession (weight index 19 to 24 for the French female population). The intergroup variation was from 19.9 to 19.3.

It was also found that global body dissatisfaction is much more discriminating (ANOVA, $p < .001$) than dissatisfaction concerning body parts ($p < .05$).

Using a series of drawings going from thin to fat (cf. Rozin, 1985), interesting results were obtained when the subjects were asked to rate themselves with reference to the figures, although the most interesting ones are trends rather than significant differences.

The majority of non-bulimics choose for themselves the figure that they had chosen as ideal for a woman, while the trend is the contrary for the bulimics. This is a very interesting result in the light of the expressed desire to lose weight in all groups. The non-bulimic group does not consider that 5 or 6 pounds above the desired weight puts them into the fat category, whereas most of the bulimics are persuaded that this is the case.

The bulimics consider themselves too fat compared to what is a desirable size for a woman and also compared to what is most attractive to men. They are however objectively normal weight.

The results of the ex-bulimics are also interesting. They no longer have a problem concerning the way they are viewed by other people, in that they no longer consider themselves too fat compared to the cultural norms, nor compared to what men appreciate. However a more personal judgement – what my real size is, and how it compares to my ideal – remain closer to those of the bulimic group than to those of the non-bulimic group. This indicates that the intimate acceptance of oneself remains vulnerable, and this may explain why so many cured bulimics relapse. An interesting finding is that, in France, two thirds of the normal-weight female population have a body image which coincides for all three measures. This corresponds more to what Rozin found for the American male population!

In fact most of the women in the global sample are either slightly happy or slightly unhappy about their body image. This may however be the result of a cultural difference between France and other countries.

CHAPTER 5

The Media Influence on Eating Problems

Glenn Waller & Julie Shaw

Both psychological theories and early research evidence
suggest that the media can influence the development
and maintenance of eating problems. Men and women
may be equally susceptible to these influences. However,
the bias in the media is towards messages advocating
thinness and dieting in women rather than in men
(Silverstein et al., 1986; Andersen & DiDomenico, 1992).
Therefore, it is likely that the influence of the media can
go part of the way towards answering the question of
why women are at particular risk of developing eating
problems. The question now is how widespread is this
influence and how can it be reduced?

Like other psychological and psychiatric disorders, eating problems are associated with a number of demographic factors. These
factors include socioeconomic status, age and race (e.g., Crisp,
Palmer & Kalucy, 1976; Mumford, Whitehouse & Platts, 1991).
However, eating problems are probably unique among functional
disorders in their gender bias. Estimates of the degree of this bias
vary substantially. However, there is no doubt that unhealthy
eating attitudes and diagnosable cases of anorexia and bulimia
nervosa are far more prevalent among women than among men. In
a review, Hsu (1989) concluded that there were approximately ten
female cases for every one male case. Rand & Kuldau's (1992)
well-controlled epidemiological study found that women showed a
much greater level of bulimic symptoms than men.

It is now widely accepted that eating problems cannot be understood in terms of single causes, and that multi-factorial models are needed (e.g., Slade, 1982; Lacey, 1986). Most of these factors (e.g., mood, personality, relationship difficulties, reinforcement) might be expected to apply equally to women and men. Even where there are gender biases in these factors (e.g., rate of depressed mood), those biases are unlikely to explain the extreme gender bias in the presence of eating psychopathology. Therefore, other factors probably need to be considered when asking why women account for such a disproportionate number of cases of anorexia and bulimia nervosa.

Sociocultural factors seem to offer the best potential explanation of why so many women suffer from eating problems. Considering the models of Slade (1982) and Lacey (1986), it appears that sociocultural influences operate in two ways – via creating a culture where slimness is valued, and by reducing perceived control over the environment. Both of these influences seem to be much more powerful among women than among men. However, it is important to consider how abstract sociocultural influences are conveyed to the individual. Among the most overt of these 'carrier mechanisms' are the mass media. The possible influence of the media has been considered widely in psychological research, although there has been little evidence of a causal relationship until recently. This research will be outlined below, but first it is important to consider theoretical viewpoints, and how they might explain the media's role in the preponderance of women suffering from eating problems.

THEORETICAL VIEWPOINTS

The primary aim of the mass media is to promote the consumption of ideas and goods. Through the ideological promotion of selected issues, the media inform girls and women what their major preoccupations should be. In particular, this 'culture of femininity' (Women's Study Group, 1978) focuses on representations of an ideal female body. For many women, such media images produce strong emotional responses, including dissatisfaction with their own bodies and the desire to attain the ultimate ideal. Such emotional responses might be among the factors that initiate the cycle of dietary restraint and binge eating which is often identified as a precursor to the development of an eating disorder (e.g., Slade, 1982; Lacey, 1986).

The peak age of onset for eating disorders is during adolescence. This stage of development is also recognized as a crucial period for gender-related identity formation. Thus, the development of female identity needs to be addressed as a central issue in theoretical formulations of the eating disorders. Personal identity is closely linked with consumer behaviour. Most people derive satisfaction and security from the social acceptance bestowed by the attainment of ideal cultural standards, which are promoted via the mass media. The acquisition of a 'designer label' or the 'perfect' body is regarded as a reflection of individual worth.

Media influences on identity formation, body image concerns and eating problems in women might be explained by theoretical perspectives drawn from the field of social psychology.

Social identity theory suggests that self-image is made up of both a personal identity and a social identity. Social identity is gained via identification with one or more social groups. A more positive social identity is associated with the increasing social desirability of the group of which one is a member. The media present images that promise or imply social acceptance for thin females, thus rendering this body type highly desirable.

Social learning theory focuses on the powerful influence of role models on the development of gender-related self-identity during childhood and adolescence. Bandura (1977) concluded that the most effective role models are those who the individual perceives as most similar to themselves. The media present role models which adolescent girls are readily able to use in their search for self-identity. Such media images are appealing because they offer a relevant focus for adolescent anxieties concerning the dramatic bodily changes during puberty. The mass media present an ideal body type for women, and image-sensitive adolescent girls experience pressure to conform to that ideal.

Social comparison theory (Festinger, 1954) suggests that there is a need to use others as a source of information about social phenomena in order to evaluate one's own abilities, attitudes, etc. . Thus, social comparison theory might explain how women use media images as a reference source in evaluating their own body image. The media's ubiquitous use of thinness as the ideal standard of bodily attractiveness for women (Silverstein, Perdue, Peterson & Kelly, 1986; Andersen & DiDomenico, 1992) is likely to cause dissatisfaction and anxiety in the large number of women whose bodies do not match this ideal.

Crit-Can I apply this?

In considering the likely effects of the media upon eating problems, three theories have been discussed – social identity theory, social learning theory and social comparison theory. However, none of these theories applies exclusively to one gender. Men are also consumers of media messages concerning the ideal male physique, yet the proportion of males who suffer eating disorders remains relatively small. Therefore, can such generic psychological theories adequately explain why women's eating might be affected by the media?

Many classic psychological theories have been described as androcentric because they fail to address female experiences as being qualitatively different to those of males. Feminist psychological theory offers a range of theoretical frameworks, which consider the numerous factors that might contribute to the development of an eating disorder. In particular, they focus on the rapidly changing, often contradictory expectations of women in contemporary Western societies. For example, Chernin (1986) has highlighted the cultural significance attached to the ideal female body, and its effect on women's relationships with food. However, although such formulations might explain increasing food and body image preoccupations amongst women, they are not sufficient to account for the development of eating disorders. It is necessary to consider the ways in which the media (and other sociocultural influences) might interact with other psychological factors in women (such as the social psychological processes outlined above) as a consequence of women's position in contemporary Western societies.

Multifactorial models of the eating disorders (e.g., Lacey, 1986) suggest that sociocultural influences interact with other factors in the development of eating problems in women. Slade's (1982) functional analysis of the eating disorders probably serves as the most useful such framework, as it suggests two specific routes through which the media may have such an influence. First, sociocultural factors can contribute to the development of a general dissatisfaction with oneself and with one's body, either directly (e.g., through messages about the importance of being slim) or indirectly (e.g., through encouraging overcontrolling parental attitudes). Slade suggests that such dissatisfaction is a key setting condition for the development of a need to control food intake. Second, sociocultural triggers can act as more immediate antecedents, triggering the initial dieting behaviour (i.e., the successful establishment of 'internal' control) that leads into the full-blown eating problem.

Slade's model is not gender-specific, so why are women's eating attitudes particularly likely to be affected by the media? The answer is probably two-fold. First, the media stress the value of bodily control far more for women than for men (Silverstein et al., 1986; Andersen & DiDomenico, 1992). Therefore, women are more likely to be dissatisfied with their 'imperfect' bodies and to seek social and personal acceptability by striving to achieve this 'ideal' goal of bodily control. Second, women are afforded fewer means of control over their own lives than men in most societies. Men who experience the same initial antecedents as women (including media pressures towards bodily control) may be able to establish control over other aspects of their own lives (e.g., at work) in ways that are less likely to be available to women.

To summarise, eating problems appear to be a manifestation of the conflicts surrounding the development of women's psychosocial identity in a society where female identity is linked substantially to body image and appearance, and where non-thinness among females is regarded as an undesirable trait. These conflicts render some women particularly sensitive to media images that portray thinness as desirable. Within Slade's (1982) model, the media may act in different ways to encourage eating psychopathology, but the gender-specific nature of these influences can only be understood within a model that considers the social factors that make women particularly likely to look upon bodily control as a means of establishing more general control over their lives. So far, this discussion has been at a theoretical level. It is necessary to see whether the prediction that the media will influence eating problems is supported, and to consider whether it might be possible to ameliorate such effects.

EMPIRICAL EVIDENCE

Having outlined the theories that suggest that the media might have an influence on eating problems, it is necessary to consider whether the existing evidence supports them. A number of studies have been conducted that examine media influences upon eating. One strand of research has presented evidence that there are historical changes in the presentation of the ideal female shape. The earliest studies focussed on the shape and size of models in

Playboy magazine and of participants in 'Miss America' contests over a number of years (e.g., Garner, Garfinkel, Schwartz & Thompson, 1980; Wiseman, Gray, Mosimann & Ahrens, 1992). These studies have shown that the ideal female shape is thin and becoming thinner. However, there are two difficulties in concluding that this finding has any bearing on the prevalence of anorexia and bulimia nervosa. First, there is only poor evidence for such an increase in prevalence, and it is more likely that the increases are due to better identification of cases. Second, there is little evidence that women are influenced by these images, which they may encounter only infrequently.

Others have conducted similar studies, concentrating on magazines, television images and models that women were likely to encounter. Silverstein et al. (1986) found strong evidence of a shift over recent decades towards a slimmer ideal in magazines and other media images, and showed that this emphasis on slimness is greater for women than for men. Morris, Cooper & Cooper (1989) concluded that fashion models were becoming more 'tubular' over time, but that this was a result of an increase in their waist sizes rather than any reduction in the size of other parts of the body. Therefore, this strand of research appears to show that there is a consistent media message extolling an ideal shape, and that this ideal is 'tubular' rather than curvaceous. However, these findings give no evidence that such a message has any effect upon its targets.

In a similar vein, there is evidence that there is an increase in media articles that encourage attention to diet (e.g., Garner, Garfinkel, Schwartz & Thompson, 1980; Wiseman, Gray, Mosimann & Ahrens, 1992). Silverstein et al. (1986) and Andersen & Di-Domenico (1992) showed that these articles are biased towards females rather than males. However, none of this research considered whether the readers' use of the media was associated with their eating attitudes and behaviours. Abramson & Valene (1991) found associations between the extent of media use and eating attitudes, but they were appropriately cautious in interpreting these correlational findings.

The general difficulty with interpreting the studies outlined above is that it is impossible to determine any causality from their correlational designs. In most cases, even the correlation is an inferred one, as no evidence is presented that the changes in media messages are associated even with the prevalence of eating problems. A small number of experimental studies have been conducted, allowing for causal inferences. Irving (1990) found that seeing photographs of thin fashion models led to a reduction in women's general self-esteem. This effect was not mediated by the woman's own bulimic eating attitudes. Hamilton & Waller (1993) showed anorexics and bulimics fashion photographs, and showed that these women overestimated their body size more after viewing these real-life images. This effect was not present in the group of comparison women as a whole, but Waller, Hamilton & Shaw (1992) showed that the effect was present for non-eating-disordered women who had more unhealthy restrictive eating attitudes. Further work has shown that there are similar effects of such media images in other groups, including adolescents (Shaw & Waller, 1993) and pregnant women (Summner, Waller, Killick & Elstein, 1994). The experimental nature of these studies and their use of real-life fashion images gives strong support to the suggestion that the media play a direct causal role as one of the factors that interact in the development of eating problems.

To summarize, it appears that the media's images have an effect upon women's self- and body-image, particularly if they already have a reason to be sensitive to their body size (eating disorder, unhealthy eating attitudes, adolescence, pregnancy). Murphy (1993) has suggested that media images also affect the self-esteem of males, although this study requires replication with a better experimental design. Such an effect in males would suggest that the same psychological links between the media messages and eating psychopathology operate in both sexes. If this link is common to males and females, then the level of messages sent to men and women advocating slimness and dieting becomes crucial. At present, those messages are directed far more at women than at men (Silverstein et al., 1986; Andersen & DiDomenico, 1992). There appears to be a danger that any increase in such messages directed at men would result in a higher prevalence of eating problems among males.

Further research is required to determine the generalizability of these conclusions (who is at risk; what media and what messages have an effect; what features of eating problems are affected). The characteristics of those who are at risk are of particular interest. These may include demographic factors, such as gender and age, but it will be of particular interest to determine the psychological characteristics of those who are most susceptible to media influences. This research should be valuable in guiding interventions.

IMPLICATIONS FOR INTERVENTION
The media have been shown to have a particular influence on women's self- and body-image. Therefore, these influences are likely to be related to general psychopathology in eating-disordered and non-eating-disordered individuals (e.g., Hartley, 1989), and it is important to consider implications for treatment. At present, any therapeutic suggestions must be entirely speculative, since there have been no attempts to modify these media effects upon eating psychopathology. There are three possible ways of producing changes that would be of benefit to the individual with an eating problem.

(a) Changing the media images and messages
If it is the case that the media causes eating psychopathology, then the simplest answer would seem to be to change the images and messages that the media broadcast. Rather than doing away with the use of slim models altogether, it would be more valuable for the media to use a much wider range of models of different sizes and shapes. This change would discourage the idealization of an unachievable form, and would encourage readers and viewers to see a wide range of body types as acceptable.

Unfortunately, this is likely to be the least feasible intervention, as the media would be resistant to such editorial constraint. The media have a number of linked objectives (such as making a profit, generating advertising, boosting circulation, art) that make it unlikely that they would agree voluntarily to produce a picture of the world as it is. The occasional changes from slimness to curvaceousness as an ideal fashionable figure is unlikely to be of benefit. Whenever a single ideal is presented, the great bulk of the population are unlikely to achieve that ideal. Unless the media are willing to promote a wider range of physical forms as acceptable, then there will continue to be an 'ideal' to which the public will aspire. Therefore, the media are likely to maintain their pathological nature, and the best course will be to attempt change at the intra-individual level.

(b) Changing the individual
At a simplistic level, one might suggest that individuals whose eating psychopathology is particularly sensitive to the media

influence should simply avoid the relevant real-life stimuli. However, this strategy is unlikely to be effective, given the all-pervading nature of these images and messages. Therefore, intervention may need to be focussed on helping the individual to change the symptoms that are exacerbated by the media. For example, a cognitive-behavioural intervention for body image distortion (e.g., Norris, 1984; Thompson, 1990) may need to be adapted to account for the role of the media in the development of cognitions about the body. However, even if such treatment were only used when the individual had a more general eating problem (and assuming that it was effective), such an intervention strategy would still require an enormous amount of clinical input. Therefore, it is unlikely to be the optimum treatment method.

(c) Preventing the media messages from having their effects

A psychoeducational approach might be the best means of reducing the media's impact on eating psychopathology. In particular, it could encourage individuals to question the validity of accepting the messages that they receive from the media. Such an intervention would probably be well suited to adolescents, and might form part of their academic curriculum. However, this approach to intervention remains untested, and so (as with the approaches outlined above) it should be treated as a possibility rather than as a recommendation at present.

REFERENCES

Abramson, E. & Valene, P. (1991). Media use, dietary restraint, bulimia and attitudes towards obesity: a preliminary study. *British Review of Bulimia and Anorexia Nervosa*, 5: 73–76.

Andersen, A.E. & DiDomenico, L. (1992). Diet vs. shape content of popular male and female magazines: A dose-response relationship to the incidence of eating disorders. *International Journal of Eating Disorders*, 11: 283–287.

Bandura, A. (1977). *Social Learning Theory*. Englewoods Cliff, NJ: Prentice-Hall.

Chernin, K. (1986). *The Hungry Self: Women, Eating and Identity*. London: Virago Press.

Crisp, A.H., Palmer, R.L. & Kalucy, R.S. (1976). How common is anorexia nervosa? A prevalence study. *British Journal of Psychiatry*, 128: 549–554.

Festinger, L. (1954). A theory of social comparison processes. *Human Relations*, 2: 117–140.

Garner, D.M., Garfinkel, P.E., Schwartz, D. & Thompson, M.(1980). Cultural expectations of thinness in women. *Psychological Reports*, 47: 483–491.

Hamilton, K. & Waller, G. (1993). Media influences on body size estimation in anorexia and bulimia: An experimental study. *British Journal of Psychiatry*, 162: 837–840.

Hartley, P. (1989) Body image and self-image in anorexia nervosa. *British Review of Bulimia and Anorexia Nervosa*, 3: 61–70

Hsu, L.K.G. (1989). The gender gap in eating disorders: Why are the eating disorders more common among women? *Clinical Psychology Review*, 9: 393–407.

Irving, L.M. (1990). Mirror images: effects of the standard of beauty on the self- and body- esteem of women exhibiting varying levels of bulimic symptoms. *Journal of Social and Clinical Psychology*, 9: 230–242.

Lacey, J.H. (1986). Pathogenesis. In: L.J. Downey & J.C. Malkin (eds.) *Current Approaches: Bulimia Nervosa*. Southampton: Duphar (pp. 17–26).

Morris, A., Cooper, T., & Cooper, P.J. (1989). The changing shape of female fashion models. *International Journal of Eating Disorders*, 8: 593–596.

Mumford, D.B., Whitehouse, A.M. and Platts, M. (1991). Sociocultural correlates of eating disorders among Asian schoolgirls in Bradford. *British Journal of Psychiatry*, 158: 222–228.

Murphy, R. (1993). The effects of observing male and female photographic models on men and women's self-esteem and body-image. Paper presented at *British Psychological Society Conference*, Blackpool, April.

Norris, D.L. (1984). The effects of mirror confrontation on self-estimation of body dimensions in anorexia nervosa, bulimia and two control groups. *Psychological Medicine*, 14: 835–842.

Rand, C.S.W. & Kuldau, J.M. (1992). Epidemiology of bulimia and symptoms in a general population: Sex, age, race, and socioeconomic status. *International Journal of Eating Disorders*, 11: 37–44.

Shaw, J. & Waller, G. (1993). Sociocultural influences on body image distortion in adolescence and adulthood: Age-specific effects of fashion magazines. *Unpublished paper under review*.

Silverstein, B., Perdue, L., Peterson, B. & Kelly, E. (1986). The role of the mass media in promoting a thin standard of bodily attractiveness for women. *Sex Roles*, 14: 519–532.

Slade, P.D. (1982). Towards a functional analysis of anorexia nervosa and bulimia nervosa. *British Journal of Clinical Psychology*, 21: 167–179.

Sumner, A., Waller, G., Killick, S., & Elstein, M. (1994). Body image distortion in pregnancy: A pilot study of the effects of media images. *Journal of Reproductive and Infant Psychology*.

Thompson, J.K. (1990). *Body Image Disturbance: Assessment and Treatment*. New York: Pergamon Press.

Waller, G., Hamilton, K. & Shaw, J. (1992). Media influences on body size estimation in eating-disordered and comparison women. *British Review of Bulimia and Anorexia Nervosa*, 6: 81–87.

Wiseman, C.V., Gray, J.J., Mosimann, J.E. & Ahrens, A.H. (1990). Cultural expectations of thinness in women: an update. *International Journal of Eating Disorders*, 11: 85–89.

Women's Studies Group (Eds.) (1978). *Women Take Issue*. London: Hutchinson (pp. 96–108).

THERAPEUTIC
APPROACHES

CHAPTER 6

Women Therapists for Women Patients?

Rose Stockwell & Bridget Dolan

In our psychodynamic work with women with bulimia we find that therapy is centred more upon the conflicts and identity struggles of being an adult woman than on the symptoms of eating behaviour. Once food abuse is dealt with behaviourally the focus of our therapeutic model is on helping the woman find an identity within her society and cultural niche. We highlight five main issues which are commonly explored in therapy with bulimic women and discuss how the personal experiences of a woman therapist may make her able offer more to the client than do the experiences of a male therapist.

In this chapter we contend that women therapists working with women with eating disorders have a extra resource which men do not have – being physically and emotionally a woman. For those working in treatment settings within the public health service, which are often short term and partly or wholly directed towards symptom relief we suggest that women therapists can capitalise on their experiences of being a woman. We feel that many clinical teams ignore rather than exploit the gender differences between their staff members in treating women with eating disorders. In part, this may be because it has not been specified in concrete terms what exactly this female gender based resource is and how it can be utilised in treatment programmes.

Women with eating disorders struggle at many different levels with conflicts related to their bodies, their capacity to have a sexually differentiated body, their sexual identity, the power of their basic drives (hunger, aggressive, destructive and sexual), which is enacted partly through their relationship with food and the way they treat their body, their identity as a woman and in their sexual relationships. We believe that where woman are entering into treatment and where unconscious processes are not going to be worked on (through exploration of transferences, defences and resistances) then women therapists will be better placed to gain the active co-operation of the client.

We also know that many women with eating disorders have suffered abusive experiences at the hands of a man and will be very wary of trusting a male therapist, no matter how sensitive he may apparently be – after all the person who was abusive was often trusted too. A female therapist will often be experienced by an abused patient as less dangerous, less abusive and more likely to understand their experiences. In the public sector, where treatments often must be short-term and cost-effective any factors which facilitate early and easy development of a fruitful therapeutic experience should be sought.

When we teach or supervise women therapists we are often asked to help them understand the specific dilemmas of women with eating disorders. The request often seems surprising as we believe that many of the issues with which their clients are struggling are versions of experiences common or familiar to most women. Through realising the universality of many of these issues women therapists may have more confidence about using their own experiences of being a woman when working with eating disordered women. We hope that this chapter will encourage women, whatever their therapeutic stance or professional discipline, to reflect upon their own experiences of being a woman. We hope too that this chapter will be of use to male workers and that personal reflection and open discussion with female colleagues will enable them to use their own male experiences more profitably.

Our wish to draw attention to therapist gender also emerged from our observation that therapist's gender, until very recently, has not been an issue in academic papers on eating disorders nor in research. Vandereycken (1993) acknowledges how 'since eating disorders occur primarily in women the *gender* of the therapist can have a substantial effect on treatment' (his italics). Several eating disorders treatment outcome studies have been reported with a wide variety of variables considered, however it is rare for a study to report on the gender of the therapists concerened. Studies have not set out to examine the efficacy of different gender therapists, nor has any treatment study specifically exploited the differences between male and female therapists. In our search of the literature we found only one experimental study that considered the issue at all. Lacey (1984) reports the impact of therapist gender on women's responses to group psychotherapy for bulimia nervosa. His study showed that there were no differences in symptomatic outcome of bulimia when groups with two female co-therapists were compared with groups with male and female co-therapists. However, the women who were treated by two female therapists said the groups were significantly more relevant to their problems and significantly more helpful than did the women treated by a male co-therapist.

We wonder if gender differences are ignored because clinicians and researchers have viewed eating disorders as a 'medical' problem. As a medical problem there would be an implication that a 'treatment' should be found that can be carried out by a professionally trained person regardless of their gender. It may be that this 'medicalisation' of eating disorders has drawn us into never questioning whether being of similar gender makes the therapist more suited to give a particular treatment or part of treatment.

In discussing the gender issue we do not presume *any* woman will be a better therapist than *any* man, or that simply being male or female can nullify any other therapeutic skills or deficits in the therapist. Indeed we concur with Vandereycken's comment, that therapists are probably better able to deal with gender related issues when they are aware of them from the outset of their work (Vandereycken, 1993). Any woman therapist who has her own agenda to work out – be it about her body image, her sexuality, her feminist views, her weight – and insists upon imposing this on the treatment of her women patients will not be helpful. Additionally, male therapists who are sensitive and attentive to the special conflicts and confusions of women with eating problems can offer their patients helpful experiences. Clearly an experienced male therapist may be better able to work with the distress of his clients than an inexperienced woman who may be overwhelmed and confused by the intensity of emotions her patients feel. For the purposes of this chapter therefore we are talking about women therapists who are not overburdened by their own agenda and who are able to bear the feelings of their patients.

For many reasons our patients have found it hard to gain understanding of themselves through their relationship with their mothers. When the woman therapist is seen to have worked out those conflicts the patient still struggles with, the therapeutic partnership can be deepened. The therapist's interactions with her woman client may give the woman a new model to identify with, or ability to strengthen aspects of herself as a woman which enables the disordered eating symptoms to be relinquished.

The therapist helps the woman patient reorganise her experience of herself often most powerfully in relationship to the present, but also in relationship to the past. In relatively short-term treatments the therapist and patient have to work on separation and differentiation rather than on dependence and mergers. For many women this represents the underpinning of the difficulty that lay in their early relationships with their mother – attempts at separation have not been successfully achieved – there is a pseudo-independence, or a clinging dependency. The woman therapist can provide a secure and nurturing relationship within the limits of the treatment programme and so give the woman client the experience of a caring relationship which neither engulfs her or shuts her out.

FUNDAMENTAL ISSUES FOR WOMEN WITH EATING DISORDERS

Most treatments available for women with eating disorders aim, in one way or another, to enable women to tolerate the thoughts, feelings, fears, and anxieties that are associated with and underlie their preoccupation with food, weight and shape. We suggest that the issues which must be commonly explored and understood in a new way by the woman are:

- food and eating
- the biological experience of being a woman
- weight, shape, and feelings about different body parts
- sexuality
- different roles as a woman

We have spelt out below how each issue arises in examples of the daily confrontations a woman with an eating disorder has with her problem. We think that most women therapists will already understand something about these issues and what make them so onerous. Particularly if she has reflected upon them for herself in an open and considered way and understands her own conflicts and difficulties. In a short paper it is impossible to be comprehensive and we aware that some of the scenarios we suggest deal with the heterosexual woman in a partnership. Whilst this precludes the experiences of many women, it does however reflect the majority of our clinical contact.

FOOD AND EATING

Despite an increasing number of men being involved in running the home, women still have far more to do with food than men. It is usually the woman who writes the shopping list, buys the food, prepares and serves most meals and deals with what remains after the meal. Each of these tasks present their own set of challenges – we will just examine shopping and leave you to think about the others. The shopping list involves money - whose money is being spent?, how much can be spent?; choice – whose needs are to be met?, whose favourites bought?, what meals are to be provided before the next shop?, what has run out and needs replacing?, should cheap alternatives be looked for and will they be adequate substitutes?, treats, low fats, low calories, cakes and biscuits or muesli bars and fruit or both?; what to buy for celebrations or disappointments or whether not to use food at all for these etc. When things go wrong with any of these processes a woman can feel it reflects upon her capabilities: if she is also attempting to recover from an eating disorder such tasks can be a nightmare.

As well as this 'here and now' confrontation with food there is also the history of our dealings with it from the moment we were born. There is the eating of food – quantity, experiences of likes and dislikes, differences between the male and female members of the family – and there is the social occasion of family meal times and our experiences here – differences between the expectations of males and females in helping prepare, serve and clear the meal, who talks at the table, who is present at meal times etc. Meal times are places where many families very concretely show gender differences.

THE BIOLOGICAL EXPERIENCE OF BEING A WOMAN

A woman worker has periods, breasts, sexual organs of reproduction and knowledge of her body's changes during her monthly cycle and her mood variations. She knows the struggles of learning to enjoy herself sexually and the difficulties in matching her chosen sexual expression or sexual orientation to societal expectations. She may have faced family planning issues – the internal examination, the decision of what form of contraception to use, the weighings at the clinic etc.

She knows her body should have the capacity to bear a child, she may have done so, actively chosen not to, or be faced with no choice through infertility. Whatever the case she will have experienced some emotions regarding motherhood. The woman therapist has her own emotional experience to draw on and help her patients name feelings and learn to talk about their bodies and their bodily experiences.

WEIGHT, SHAPE AND FEELINGS ABOUT DIFFERENT BODY PARTS
Research repeatedly informs us that women are concerned about their weight – most women, when asked, say they would like to be at least a kilogram or two lighter. Many women also have personal concerns and conflicts about their shape, about parts of their body being 'wrong', about what they wear and about how they look.

Women therapists have first hand experience of the dilemmas about wieght and body which face their clients: of shared changing rooms; of wondering what to wear; of wondering what to do (if anything) about hairy legs, armpits and the pubic line; of shops that never sell the clothes that suit you; etc. Even those women therapists who choose not to accept social stereotypes of femininity have knowledge of the social 'norms' they are refusing to accept.

SEXUALITY
Our feelings and attitudes to our sexuality are closely linked to how we feel about our bodies and how we present ourselves not only through our clothes but our whole manner. It is closely tied up with our experiences through childhood of our own sexual development and that of parents sexual relationship and those of our brothers and sisters. These early experiences and our adult ones will effect our feelings about masturbation and sexual relationships and our capacity to enjoy our own sexuality fully. For many women with eating disorders accepting their sexuality, regardless of its orientation, is a paramount issue. Although men therapists also must deal with their own male sexuality this does not replace the intuitive and integrated sense of how women's sexuality feels for a woman.

CHAPTER 7

Can Women with Eating Disorders Benefit from a Male Therapist?

Werner Köpp

Although the majority of those who suffer with eating disorders are female the issue of whether their therapists should also be female is just beginning to be explored. This paper highlights several issues relating to therapist gender and considers the pros and cons of both male and female therapists when working with eating disordered women. It is suggested that although clients should have a choice of the gender of their therapist there are potential problems with both women and men. Ideally the therapist should be supervised by someone of the opposite gender and attention should be made to transferential and countertransferential problems.

CAN WOMEN WITH EATING DISORDERS BENEFIT FROM A MALE THERAPIST?

One could easily answer 'Yes'. However, in that doing so we would not have understood the implications of this question or the conditions under which this simple answer might be right or wrong.

If we accept Freud's recommendation (1912), the ideal therapist should be like a mirror reflecting only what the patient is showing. If a therapist could really fulfill this requirement, we would not even need to ask the above question. Gender of therapist would become immaterial as every aspect of transference would appear during a regular analysis.

There are, however, two important caveats to consider: Firstly, the therapy of patients with eating disorders usually is not a regular psychoanalysis. Secondly, more recent analytical writings on countertransference suggest that the analyst's 'personal equation' and the analyst's personality structure are of great importance in the process of psychotherapy (Riemann, 1960, 1964). Thus, the 'reflective capacity' of the analyst or therapist 'as a mirror' is limited because of his/her personality. Undoubtedly, the therapist's sex plays a role for both transference and counter-transference. Up till now we can only hypothesise about what role gender plays in therapy and whether it influences only the process or also the outcome of that therapy.

In recent years, feminist therapists have been suggesting fundamental changes in common types of therapy. Rejecting the techniques of behavioural and analytical treatment (Burgard, 1986), they propagate a new therapeutical approach (Mies, 1978) which includes:

- identification with the female patient
- clearly evident preference for the female patient
- equality and equilibrium between the therapist and her female patient.

Without using psychoanalytical terms, Scheffler (1986) emphasises that inequality between female patients and female therapists has to be analysed and made transparent as an 'example of the female's inferior position which creates her dependency and her helplessness'.

To exemplify feminist therapy, Burgard (1986) presents a very interesting case report of a woman (not suffering from eating disorders) in treatment with a female analyst. The female therapist is seen as supporting her patient to gain some power of her own or perhaps to 'score points' off her friend. It is impressive how aspects of inequality between the therapist and her patient are taken into consideration. On the other hand, the therapist rejects any idea of the patient's masochism although the patient has lived with a boyfriend maltreating her for more than five years. Feelings of shame and guilt towards this man are not interpreted by the female therapist as intrapsychic problems but as being attributable to societal conditions hostile to women, which are experienced by the female patient and her therapist alike.

Regardless of one's own agreement with this view, we should not cut off the discussion with feminist therapists at this point. This feminist approach, considering the psycho-social aspects of the culture in which women live alongside the clients intrapsychic status, have been neglected in conventional types of therapy for many years. We should perhaps accept these aspects as being important without losing the intrapsychic perspective.

FEMALE OR MALE THERAPIST?

In regard to the question of whether female patients with eating disorders can benefit from male therapists, there is very little evidence that patients can benefit less or more with a female therapist than with a male therapist. Lacey (1985) emphasises that in his opinion the therapist's gender influences only the process of therapy rather than the final outcome. He notes that the therapist's gender seems to have a greater effect in group therapy than in individual sessions. While groups with a male and female therapists seem to concentrate more on the parental marital conflicts, the all female groups tend to concentrate on relationships with mothers in a way which the presence of a man precludes.

Various arguments for the standpoint that female therapists are preferable for female patients with eating disorders are collected below.

- Anorexia and bulimia are typically female disorders and can therefore be understood better by female therapists.
- Female therapists are less offensive and have more empathy; they handle therapeutic rules and methods in a more pragmatic way (Gürtler, 1987).
- Women have more 'female intuition'. They try to demonstrate their power rather than their weakness (Baker-Miller, 1979). Therefore, female patients need not be afraid to lose closeness in a relationship with a female therapist if they show their weakness and their power (Gürtler, 1987).
- Female therapists' reactions are more sensitive; female therapists perceive more of the feelings expressed by their patients and also show more of their own feelings than their male counterparts (Orlinsky et al., 1969).
- Given that the gender relationship in our society is one of male dominance, if a female patient is treated by a male therapist,

there is a considerable danger of a second dominance within the therapeutic relationship.

There are, however, other arguments indicating that male therapists could be as good as female therapists – or perhaps even better:

- Female therapists run the risk of acting out their over-identification with their patient.
- Some female patients idealise their female therapists. This idealisation in its extreme form could lead to psychological self-destruction because the patients develop a feeling of inferiority by not being able to reach their ideal.
- A male therapist offers a better chance to work out the Oedipal conflict.
- Personal identity develops by experiencing separateness and autonomy. The opposite sex of the therapist could be conducive to this process.
- The gender relationship in our society is one of male dominance and female subordination. A therapeutic approach for the female patient is easier with a male therapist because analysis of transference and countertransference helps the patient develop realistic new coping styles.

WHY CHOOSE A WOMAN THERAPIST?

According to Symonds (1976), Turkel (1976) and Person (1986), female patients in urban centers tend to prefer female therapists. Person claims that we must accept that changes in values and perceptions dictate dramatically different adaptations, choices and solutions of conflicts. She suggests motives for a woman choosing a therapist of the same sex, summed up under four different headings:

- A fear that a male therapist will hold on to sexist values.
- A belief that it is too easy and tempting to fool a male therapist and thereby avoid problematic topics.
- The wish to avoid an erotic transference or countertransference.
- The explicit desire to have a strong, competent woman with whom to make a positive identification.

Based on her activity as a training analyst and supervisor, she presents a clinical vignette which illustrates that common biases – sexism included – can destroy the therapeutic process. On the other hand, regardless of gender, a therapist free of values is an impossible ideal and we must assume that the therapist's interventions and interpretations are also not value free. This must be equally true of female therapists.

Person (1986) detects a transferential pitfall for male therapists, illustrating in a case report how a female patient 'did' treatment for her therapist in the same way that she 'did' sex for her husband. Person considered this behaviour in therapy as being symbolically linked to faking orgasm. Gradually, the patient began to complain that treatment was empty despite her seeming ability to make associations, utilise interpretations and so forth.

Person also refers to Zetzel's statement (1966) that especially in short-term therapies, the female patients' wish for a role model leads to a positive transference and identification which should be regarded as a valid psychotherapeutic goal. In her opinion it is impossible to judge the impact of the therapist's gender on the therapy's result.

Meyers (1986) raises the important question whether it is not an unrealistic expectation that a female therapist could understand her female patient better. According to her, it could also be an idealisation that more and more female patients are being referred to female therapists. The idea behind is that certain issues may not have been touched with a male therapist but will come to the fore in the transference with a woman. She claims that in a complete analysis it does not matter whether the therapist is a man or a woman; but in her opinion 'the therapist's gender affects sequence, intensity, and certain transference paradigms in both therapy and analysis. Certainly, the earliest transference reactions tend to be influenced by the therapist's gender, as well as by other reality factors'.

SHOULD CLIENTS HAVE THE CHOICE OF THERAPIST'S GENDER?

Person supports Greenacre's standpoint (1959) 'If a little discussion indicates that this is a definitely established attitude of the patients, I myself always treat it with the utmost respect and compliance, since I recognise that such a patient really would find it difficult, if not impossible, to work with an analyst of the undesired sex'. For the therapy of women with eating disorders, her view of transferential and countertransferential aspects related to the gender of the therapist seems to be of great value. The participants of a workshop on the therapist's gender at the 'Why Women?' conference (in Ulm, 1990) joined this discussion with further considerations.

They stated that it is no use making generalisations about the therapist's gender in the therapy of women with eating disorders. Also, in many clients who have experienced sexual abuse the fantasies and feelings related to the therapist's gender are possibly more important than in others. A positive transference at the beginning of the therapy was considered most important. Therefore, the patient should be asked – especially in hospitals, where the patient does not always have the choice of her therapist – whether the therapist's gender is of any importance for her.

It was stated that empathy is necessary for any type of therapy with women who have eating disorders. On the other hand, over empathising could be a pitfall which leads to a situation where there is no room for conflict. The patient's ability to disagree with her therapist was considered a very important step forward in the course of therapy.

Transferential and countertransferential problems may occur in therapies with both male and female therapists. As an ideal neutral attitude of the therapist is not possible, some remarkable claims not yet discussed in the literature were made:-

- No therapist should treat any woman with eating disorders without supervision.
- If the therapist is male, the main supervising person should be female (and vice versa).
- If the therapy of a woman with eating disorders seems to become impossible in the patient's view because of gender related transferential problems, a change of the therapist should be considered.

Any consideration in such a situation should concentrate upon the question 'what enables the patient to start or to continue the therapy?' In this context, issues of defense mechanisms and resistance are of secondary importance to the practical issue of keeping the client engaged in therapy.

Self-help Groups for Women with Bulimia 71

REFERENCES
Baker-Miller, J. (1976) *Toward a new psychology of woman.* Beacon, Boston. German trans: *Die Stärke weiblicher Schwäche.* Fischer, Frankfurt/Main (1979)
Burgard R. (1986) Warum brauchen wir feministische Therapie? *Beiträge zur feministischen Theorie und Praxis,* 9(17): 41–52
Freud S. (1912) Ratschläge für den Arzt bei der psychoanalytischen Behandlung *Gesammelte Werke,* 8, Fischer, Frankfurt/Main (1973), 384
Greenacre P. (1959) Certain technical problems in the transference relationship. *Journal of American Psychoanalytic Association.* 7: 484–502
Gürtler H. (1987) Arbeiten Therapeutinnen anders? Der Einfluß des Geschlechts auf das therapeutische Verhalten. In: Rommelspacher P. (Ed.): *Weibliche Beziehungsmuster.* Campus, Frankfurt/Main
Lacey J.H. (1985) Time-limited individual and group treatment for bulimia. In: Garner D.M. and Garfinkel (Ed.): *Handbook of Psychotherapy for Anorexia and Bulimia.* Guilford, New York-London
Meyers H.C. (1986) Analytic work by and with women. The complexity and the challenge. In: Meyers H.C. (Ed.): *Between analyst and patient: Dimensions in countertransference and transference.* The Analytic Press, Hillsdale/New Jersey.
Mies M. (1978) Methodische Postulate zur Frauenforschung (cited by Burgard)
Orlinsky D.E., Howard K.I., Hill J.A. (1969) The therapist's feelings in the psychotherapeutic process. *Journal of Clinical Psychology,* 25: 83-93
Person E.S. (1986) Women in therapy: therapist gender as a variable. In: Meyers H.C. (op.cit.)
Racker H.(1959). *Übertragung und Gegenübertragung. Studien zur psychoanalytischen Technik.* Reinhardt, München-Basel (1982)
Riemann F. (1960) Bedeutung und Handhabung der Gegenübertragung. *Zeit. für Psychosomatische Medicin,* 6(2): 123–132
Riemann F. (1964) Die Struktur des Analytikers und ihr Einfluß auf den Behandlungsverlauf. In: Salzmann L., Schwidder W., Westerman Holstijn A.J. (Ed.). *Fortschritte der Psychoanalyse Bd. 1,* Hogrefe, Göttingen.
Scheffler S. (1986) Feministische Therapie. *Beiträge zur feministischen Theorie und Praxis,* 9(17): 25–40
Symonds A. (1976) Neurotic dependency in successful women. (cited by Person)
Turkel A.R. (1976) The impact of feminism on the practice of a woman analyst (cited by Person)
Zetzel E.R. (1970) The doctor-patient relationship in psychiatry. (cited by Person).

CHAPTER 8

Self-help Groups for Women with Bulimia Nervosa

Jennifer Munro & Malcolm Laing

The development of a self-help group for women suffering from bulimia nervosa in Edinburgh is described. This self-help group arose when clients participating in a therapist-led group treatment programme for bulimia nervosa expressed a need for further support. The self-help group was developed in conjunction with the clinic's own long-term follow-up groups. The aim of the self-help group was to encourage all clients who had completed the therapy group to continue to tackle their bulimic symptoms whilst also further developing supportive relationships within a group setting. The self-help group is therefore exclusive to women who have completed a treatment programme in the clinic. This chapter discusses our experiences of the value of this group and also addresses some of the difficulties that have arisen in its development.

The value of self-help for bulimia nervosa has become more apparent as the number of sufferers appears to be on the increase in the Western World. The few papers on self-help suggest that it has an important role in providing support to women with eating disorders who have not responded to medical or psychiatric treatment or who do not wish to approach professionals for help (Deeble et al., 1990; Malenbaum et al., 1988). In addition to this they can provide an excellent supportive system for the relatives and friends of someone suffering from an eating disorder. However, it could be argued that women who have benefited from treatment may also be able to make good use of community based self-help groups. This is particularly the case in busy health service settings where facilities for long term support are often not available.

It is well recognised that a follow-up treatment period of at least twelve months is required to facilitate any permanent changes (Oesterheld, 1987; Hsu,1986). The symptoms of bulimia nervosa tend to recur in times of stress and we have found women tend to attribute a recurrence of symptoms as 'relapse' and therefore 'failure'. This very negative interpretation of the process of bulimia is detrimental to the client's overall recovery. Therefore in dealing with this chronic, fluctuating disorder, it is important for both client and therapist to forsee the limitations of therapy. A client may do extremely well within the safety of a therapeutic relationship but this does not necessarily protect her from future difficulties and therefore a recurrence of symptoms should never be deemed a failure.

One way of assisting women to continue to tackle their bulimia after treatment is to encourage them to support each other outside the clinic. This may be more pertinent to a group therapy as relationships have already been established between the women. As yet the value of self-help as a progression from group therapy has not been fully examined.

This chapter explores the role of self-help for women after a formal therapy group has been completed. It is based on our own experiences of helping women to organise meetings out-with the therapy setting. The self-help has therefore evolved as an adjunct to the psycho-educational group packages run in the unit. These groups are the main treatment for bulimia nervosa in our Edinburgh clinic due to the very high referral rate. To date, seventeen groups have now run exclusively for women. In the last year a pilot study for a similar group for men has commenced but there has not yet been enough referrals of male clients with bulimia to allow for a satisfactory male/female balance within the groups.

The facility in the clinic is known as the 'Bulimia First Aid Group'. Its remit is to teach alternative coping strategies to replace binge eating and vomiting with a major emphasis on self-help and mutual support. The group is closed and offers a two year package with three phases; – the initial intensive phase comprises twelve weekly sessions; phase two is the follow-up groups held one month after the end of phase one and then at three-monthly intervals. The third phase is the use of self-help in the community.

This third phase was initiated by some of the women who had completed the first twelve weeks of therapy. They expressed a need to continue to tackle their symptoms whilst exploring some of the broader issues around their eating disorder. They were enthusiastic about setting up a self-help group for these reasons and the therapists were in agreement that this could be a positive therapeutic step. It was felt that the transition into self-help could be well supported by the phase two follow-up groups and hopefully would also encourage a higher sustained attendance at these important therapy follow-ups.

After discussion and some guidance from the therapists, the women drew up the following aims for their self-help group:

- As a forward progression from therapist-led groups
- To encourage continued mutual support
- To allow for exploration of broader issues around eating disorders

The therapists in the clinic provided practical guidance and support to the women whilst they set up their group. The women then invited themselves to each consecutive therapy group as it reached the end of phase one. In this way clients were encouraged to join the community-based support group after they had completed their twelve weeks of intensive treatment. Although a selection of different venues were tried it was eventually decided to alternate the meetings around the group members' homes as this proved to be the most successful option.

The group has been running for three years now and has not been without difficulties. The main aims of this discussion are to address some of the areas of difficulty. Most of the literature on self-help would suggest that there are always problems in organising self-help groups of any kind so we have considered issues that may be of particular relevance to women setting up a group for bulimia nervosa.

The following issues are explored:

- The transition from the clinic to the community
- Sharing responsibility for running the group
- Coping with group dynamics
- Losing the support of the therapist
- Client's motivation towards self-help
- Outlining realistic goals & expectations

THE TRANSITION FROM THE CLINIC TO THE COMMUNITY

Women suffering from bulimia nervosa are usually seen to be coping well in the eyes of others. A sufferer may hold down a prestigious job, be seen to have an enviable social life and be involved in sexual relationships. She somehow succeeds in portraying an image of herself that conceals all the internal distress from her friends and family members.

We have found that many women who have requested professional help for their eating disorder find it easier to disclose and address their symptoms in an environment that is clearly removed from everyday life. However, we believe that an important contributing factor to the symptoms of bulimia is the sufferer's apparent need to portray herself as a flawless, caring, coping female. This image appears to act as a protection against exposure of the woman's underlying poor self image and fragile self-esteem. Society's role in perpetuating this conflict between the woman's real self and her image is explored fully in Chapter 2 by Weeda-Mannak.

We feel that recovery from the eating disorder requires the sufferer to fully accept and confront her eating disorder out-with the safety and secrecy of the clinic. This can be an uncomfortable experience for her as it requires her to inform others of some of her difficulties and weaknesses in order to break away from this perfect image and allow her real self to be exposed and accepted. This fear of exposure causes many women to experience a high degree of anxiety about attending a self-help group in the community but we feel it is a valuable step towards self acceptance.

SHARING RESPONSIBILITY FOR RUNNING THE GROUP

The need to attain a perfect image makes many women feel that they ought to be able to take on responsibility for all sorts of things in their lives. They therefore believe that shunning responsibility is attributable to a personal failure.

In order for a self-help group to be effective, openness regarding issues of responsibility is essential. Individuals must be aware of the potential difficulties they can experience when taking or sharing the responsibility of self-help groups. Noble (1987) suggests that responsibility is rotated equally around the women in her description of a compulsive eaters group. This may be an effective strategy but has so far proven to be difficult to implement in reality in our Edinburgh group.

It seems inevitable that some women will take on more responsibility than others. Women in this position will at times, have needs
that require them to let go of this responsible role and the other
members have to be vigilant to this in order to provide appropriate
support.

COPING WITH GROUP DYNAMICS

We have found that within the short space of the intensive group
therapy, women have been able to confront and address many
important inter-personal issues arising in the group. We were
concerned however, that the women moving on to the self-help
group may feel more uneasy about dealing with the group dynamics
without the therapists' help in recognising and guiding feelings.
However it appears that the anxieties about not coping with these
issues were worse than the reality. The group members were quick
to deal with problems such as issues around responsibility, jealousy
and control and indeed realised the importance of open, honest
relationships for the survival of the group.

LOSING THE SUPPORT OF THE THERAPIST

After establishing a relationship in therapy of any sort it is important for the client and therapist to work together towards termina-
tion of treatment. This may pose a problem in a group setting
where there is less time to spend on an individual's personal
feelings about leaving intensive therapy. Although it is fully stressed
in our group treatment that clients are expected to make gradual
changes throughout all the phases, some of the women feel that
they are only beginning to make progress by the end of the twelve
weeks and feel that their needs for more input and support may
not be met by self-help.

It is tempting for a therapist at this stage to respond to the
feelings of 'not giving enough' by adding extra appointments but
this does not encourage the bulimic woman to discover that she is
responsible for her own progress and recovery. The self-help group
can, given the chance, provide an opportunity for discovering
autonomy and independence in overcoming an eating disorder.

CLIENTS' MOTIVATION TOWARDS SELF-HELP

In our group, it appeared that each woman's response to treatment
was probably highly related to her motivation towards self-help.

Women who are symptom free by the end of the first phase sometimes reject the opportunity to use the self-help group. This may be due to their desire to get on with their lives without the reminder of their eating disorder behind them. However it is helpful for these women to be encouraged to realise that bulimic symptoms tend to recur in times of stress and that support from the self-help group can help them overcome any future difficulties.

In our experience, the women who make best use of the self-help facility have made some progress towards reducing their symptoms and yet feel they have underlying issues still to address before overcoming their problems. It is important for them to always remember that they have made progress and for them to acknowledge any difficulties they may experience in losing the support of structured therapy.

The small proportion of women who make no progress or who become worse through therapy tend not to attend the self-help phase. It should be stressed to them that recovery from bulimia is a long, slow painful process. It may be that they will be able to use the experiences of therapy at a later date and the self-help group can assist by providing continued support and encouragement throughout this time.

OUTLINING EXPECTATIONS AND GOALS
One of the problems we experience in our group treatment is that high expectations for a complete recovery are created from the onset of therapy. This is may be a result of both the therapist's and the client's difficulty in accepting that therapy cannot produce lasting changes in bulimic symptoms without a great deal of motivation from the sufferer herself over a prolonged period of time. We in fact, find ourselves questioning our treatment for bulimia nervosa far more than for other problems seen in the clinic. This is probably because we find it hard to accept the difficulties in treating bulimia successfully and permanently. There is often a strong feeling from our clients of wanting to be 'cured' yet the reality is that recovery depends on the woman's own resourcefulness and determination to deal with her problems out-with the therapy office and we can only encourage and guide her towards this.

We would therefore advise that the expectations of a self-help group are drawn out carefully at the start, and the following questions addressed;

- Is the group for support only or is there an expectation that it develops as the group members actively attempt to overcome their difficulties together?
- How structured is the group going to be? Will there be themes for each meeting or will it be open unstructured meetings?
- Are there specific aims and goals and if so is everyone going to be able to work towards to the same goals?
- If not, will some members become isolated from others because they are seen to be making less progress?
- Is there enough flexibility within the group for members to make changes at their own speed?

SUMMARY

When this project was first proposed three years ago we predicted that the women might feel uneasy about progressing to self-help without the therapists being available to recognise and guide feelings created within the group.

The group does remain small in numbers but those who have committed themselves to it have succeeded in confronting their fears about sharing their experiences out-with the clinic. In addition to this they have continued to provide an on-going and valued support system for themselves and others suffering from bulimia nervosa.

REFERENCES

Deeble E., Crisp A., Lacey J.H. & Bhat A. (1990) A Comparison Between Women Seeking Self-Help and Psychiatric Treatment in Anorexia Nervosa and Bulimia. *British Journal of Medical Psychology*, 63: 65–72.

Hsu G. & Holder D. (1986) Bulimia Nervosa, Treatment and Short Term Outcome. *Psychological Medicine*, 16: 65–70.

Malenbaum R., Herzog D., Gisenthal S. & Wyshak G. (1988) Overeaters Anonymous, Impact on Bulimia. *International Journal of Eating Disorders*, 7: 139- 145.

Noble K. (1987) Self-Help Groups: The Agony and the Ecstacy, in Lawrence M. *Fed Up and Hungry*, 115–135, Women's Press.

Oesterheld J., McKenna M. & Gould N. (1987) Group Psychotherapy of Bulimia: A Critical Review. *International Journal of Group Therapy*, 37(2): 163- 185.

CHAPTER 9

Psycho-social Factors in Eating Disorders Explored through Psychodrama and Art Therapy

Mary Levens

It is well established that there exist significant social as well as psychological factors contributing to the aetiology or maintenance of the eating disorders, anorexia nervosa and bulimia (Dana & Lawrence, 1988; Eichenbaum & Orbach, 1985). However, it remains a challenge for the analytically oriented therapist to keep in mind at all times, the social and cultural context, within which an individual's (or group's) abundant internal psychic material presents itself. All therapists, are not only responding to their client's personal communications, but bring to the therapeutic relationship, their own cultural history, which interacts with that of their clients. How some of these issues may be of particular relevance to working with sufferers of eating disorders in art therapy and psychodrama, and in what ways they may be highlighted in order to be worked with and through, is the subject of this chapter.

Art therapy and Psychodrama are an integral part of the in-patient treatment programme for eating-disordered patients at the Atkinson Morley's Hospital, London. Two case illustrations will be presented, the first, describing a psychodrama session with an anorectic woman, the second, an art therapy session with a woman suffering from bulimia nervosa.

Psychodrama is a form of group psychotherapy developed by Moreno (his particular philosophy is well described by Fox, 1987).

One member of the group, in each psychodrama session has the opportunity to explore an issue of their choice. The techniques involve finding concrete means of expression for the internal world, this may be a significant relationship with another person, or even the relationship between parts of the self can be examined. Women with eating disorders often choose to work on their hatred of their body, their fear of sexuality or conflicts concerning food and eating.

Each session comprises of a number of scenes which are enacted by the woman (known as the protagonist) with the help of other group members, taking on significant roles. Psychodrama enhances the imagination, using humour and spontaneity as part of its surgical kit. Allowing access to significant aspects of the person's internal world which can be concretized and given a voice. Our internal world exists through a series of inner relationships, which are constantly being played out as internal mini-dramas, effecting our feelings and behaviours. The various self perceptions we carry around, which alter according to the context, also effect our overt behaviour. It is these dynamic issues which come to be portrayed within a psychodrama session, each scene attempting, with the help of the therapist (the 'director'), to deepen the exploration of the protagonist's work.

Typically, each scene will reach farther and farther back into the protagonist's history, allowing her to re-experience and thereby rediscover her past. Much of the therapeutic work of the session, occurs located back in the protagonist's childhood, where the necessary but faulty protective mechanisms were originally established. Within the session, the protagonist is helped to find alternative ways of managing what originally could not be managed and this experiential learning is then brought forward into the present day situation.

I have selected a few scenes from a whole session, which highlight certain important issues to do with generational patterns of relating and some of the specific issues concerning womens' roles. The woman, Ann, is a 22 year old nanny, who had been reluctantly taken to her G.P. by her employers who were very concerned about her dramatic weight loss and refusal to eat with the family. Ann had previously been diagnosed as suffering from anorexia nervosa in her teens and had been admitted as a medical emergency for life saving measures at that time. She had however refused any offer of psychological help until this present time. Her parents led separate rather isolated lives and Ann had often accompanied her mother to social events which her father was not interested in attending. There was a much older brother with whom Ann had practically no contact, as he had split himself off to a large extent from the rest of the family.

Ann's relationship with their father somewhat mimicked that of her mother's, a relationship characterised by passivity and sub-servience; in relation to both her parents, Ann had been unable to assert her own or any different ideas. She joined the psychodrama group, after a number of months of hospitalisation, during which time she reached her 'target weight'. In this session she said she would like to explore her relationship with her mother, in particular her difficulty in saying 'No' to her.

In the initial scene Ann chose to recreate a family meal, which had occurred the previous week, at which she had been unable to say 'No' to her mothers insistent offers of further helpings of food. In this scene we used a psychodramatic 'double', that is, another member from the group who sat next to Ann, helping her to express those things she found difficult. So whilst in the scene, Ann accepted the food from her mother, her double was shouting.

'You know I can't say NO to you, if you make me eat this you know I'm going to have to get rid of it afterwards'.

When Ann is asked to swop chairs with her mother, so that she now takes on the role of her own mother, she is invited to respond to this accusation. In role as mother, Ann says,

'I want to be a good mother to you, I love you, I just want to show you that I care about you'.

The therapist (director) interviews 'mother' still played by Ann.

Director: 'Could you tell us about your idea of being a good mother to Ann?'
'Mother': 'I want her to be able to think of me as her best friend as well as her mother, I never had that with my own mother, I wish I had'.
Director: 'Could you talk to Ann about that'.
'Mother': 'I don't understand this anorexia Ann, you've had absolutely everything anyone could have wanted, I don't feel that we've gone wrong anywhere, we love you. I wouldn't have

even been able to imagine having half the opportunities that are open to you, when I was your age'.

As director, a number of possibilities have opened themselves up for further exploration. The director is aware of Ann's typical anorectic external compliance, the outer self that suggests there is little inner autonomous self able to either differentiate her own wishes from those of her mother, or if able to do so, fearful of the imagined aggressive attack, inherent in standing up for herself and rejecting an offer from her mother. In other words, establishing some tentative boundaries. The external compliance, however masks a disguised form of controlling the whole family, for instance in her usual domination of the kitchen.

This family meal, where mother was trying to prove her worth through the food she offered, held within it the family's history of Ann having usurped mother's traditional role, hardly letting her in the kitchen as she had taken full control of food supplies, prior to her hospital admission. Therefore there was also an unspoken power battle going on between mother and daughter as to who was able to be the controller of food. The kitchen had become the symbol of manipulation and power. What was also to become evident throughout this session was the ambiguity of both women's feelings for each other. This mother had not had sufficient mothering herself. In fact her history was of being brought up during the war, with food rationing and experiencing both physical and emotional deprivation. The initial hints at the mother's envy of her daughter's opportunities, were to unfold into a myriad of unconscious attacks on the notion of success.

Ann was later to discover that her chosen career reflected one way in which she need not set her aims above those of her mother. In the absence of being able to venerate her mother's position by imitating it through childrearing, becoming a nanny would presently suffice. What became evident when Ann stayed in role as her own mother for some time, and therefore expressed her internal perception of that role, was a subtle but ongoing rejection of any of the daughter's independent achievements. When Ann was asked to reverse back into taking on her own role once more and could hear these statements, said out loud by another group member now taking on the role of mother, she became aware of her true compliant act having been to go along with this rejection of certain parts of herself.

The director invites 'mother', played once more by Ann, to go back in time and have the opportunity to talk to her own mother, (ie: Ann's grandmother who in reality is now dead). In this scene a group member is selected to play grandmother, after the group is informed of her significant characteristics. 'Mother' is given the chance to have a conversation she had never had.

> *'Grandmother':* 'Nothing I did was ever good enough for you, I did everything a mother could, and then you turn round and tell me I wasn't close enough to you. What else could I have done'?
> *'Mother':* 'I didn't want you to do so much for me, that just made me feel guilty and endeared to you'.

The director is aware that through the roles of mother and grandmother, Ann is able to approach areas which are at present unacceptable to her in relation to her own mother. However, she comes to see through this session that the historical legacy that has been passed down to her belongs at least to these three generations of women. At this point, Ann is so overwhelmed with guilt at the thought of any conflict with her mother, that starvation acts as due punishment. Ann needs to discover her fears of separation and abandonment. She has been her mother's partner, in lieu of mother's own mother and currently, her absent husband. The enmeshed pair have been functioning as an embittered-sweet couple. Ann's lack of differentiation from her mother leads to severe difficulties in functioning autonomously in her internal world, who is it that is going to be abandoned? Socially, we can see that there are sufficient pressures on Ann within the family system to remain partnered to mother, and historically, it becomes clear that there is an established and continuing role for the women in the family to stay deprived but indebted to their mothers.

> *'Mother':* 'You didn't like it when I married Simon, but why shouldn't I lead my own life?'
> *'Grandmother':* 'I don't know why I bothered, you always threw everything back in my face'.

A row develops between the two characters (mother played at this point by Ann). The director thinks about the repetition of this theme, for the mother, her fight for independence being expressed through an early 'unsuitable' marriage, Ann's battle remaining indirectly expressed through her anorexia. Grandmother is hurt and rejected by her daughter's wish to separate (now played by Ann, so that what is being portrayed comes from Ann's own unconscious fantasies of her historical roots). Grandmother is undoubtedly wounded by what emerges next, which is her daughter's opportunity, (which she never took up due to her marriage) to study medicine. Grandmother's reaction to these opportunities newly open to her daughter is one of envy and confusion. Her envy results in her belittling attempts to curtail her daughter's freedom, and we see how mother also unconsciously complied with the message, 'Thou shalt not become successful and independent', by choosing to reject the offer of following a career of her own. Grandmother's confusion surrounds her problem in identifying with her own daughter who is questioning her traditional role as wife and mother by contemplating something more.

Ann is then asked to observe two other group members to play out this scene. The degree to which the issues reflect historical accuracy is not the question, the scenes have been created by a dramatisation of Ann's internal object relationships. She is able to perceive that the world which she inhabits, is closely identified with that of her mother's, so that she conceives of autonomy and independence as a wounding rejection of not only her mother as an individual, but also of the role of mother. She has tried to compensate for this perceived 'attack' by partially identifying with the mothering role, although her work as a nanny also represents her wish to stay locked within a carer-child relationship, where she can unconsciously also identify with the cared for children.

In a final scene, Ann decides to meet her mother again, and says to the director that she does not want to stay stuck in 'the same old guilt trap'. Another member plays mother.

> *Ann:* 'You know, I feel guilty every time I achieve anything, it feels like you're going to be so hurt by it (a sudden realisation). I think I might even have failed my A level examinations because I was scared to pass'.

The director thinks the enactment is helping Ann to conceptualise the possibility of difference, the idea of her and her mother co-existing with their own separate lives. Ann becomes tearful but continues.

Ann: 'There's a lot I'd really like to do with my life but that doesn't mean I don't want you to be my mother'.

The director closes the scene by bringing it round full circle to the original starting scene where Ann was unable to refuse a second helping of food, and encourages her to make a statement at this point to her mother.

Ann: 'I want to be able to say I've had enough to you Mum, without you getting so hurt. I know I have to eat correctly otherwise I get myself into serious trouble, I can't afford to stay locked into what used to happen'.

The scene is ended at this point. The group gather together and participants de-role. The session ends with each member sharing with Ann how they could identify with her work.

The theme of the session is interestingly described in a book entitled 'The Pregnant Virgin', where the author states.

'The negative mother complex will not want her to accomplish anything for herself. That would be selfish. Only giving is safe. What she has to see is that giving can be rank manipulation. Moreover, the complex interprets receiving as being manipulated ... If she can bring the negative mother to consciousness and realise that it is the complex that will not allow her to achieve, 'because it isn't nice to be ambitious', then she can stop deceiving herself and decide whether she wants to write the paper or whether she never wanted to go to University in the first place.' (Woodman, 1985)

Art therapy is another means of helping the person to discover and find external expression to their inner world. Thoughts and feelings derived from the unconscious often reach expression in images rather that words, art therapy allows this to be used as an alternative language, perhaps when words are too restrictive, or alternatively when words are used defensively by an articulate person. The therapist explores with the person, elements of the art work, such as colour, space and form and particularly their own associations to what has been produced.

After the production of images, which are created as spontaneously as possible, the therapist and individual or group explore together, the fantasies emerging from the work, the order the various images were produced in, why and when certain alterations were made and the way in which the work was produced. The resulting images are only relevant, in so far the person is in an active relationship with them, and in that way they reflect her individual conscious and unconscious meanings as well as carrying social and cultural meanings.

The issue of the dichotomy of language is raised by the work of art therapy. On the one hand the individual may be highly articulate, and yet simultaneously lacking in an emotional vocabulary. In relation to women's language we can ask if there is a gender related silencing of certain concepts and words which women have been socialised into not verbalising? This next part concerning emotions some women have difficulty expressing and why that might be the case.

Lee is 28. She works for a prestigious advertising company and is a sociable, gregarious person. Due to her intense shame, she had not revealed the fact that she has a ten year history of severe bulimia, bingeing and vomiting at least 4–6 times a day, and using 150 laxatives daily on admission. She also cut herself regularly and used a variety of means of self-harm. She would compulsively shoplift, stealing shiny trinkets which she claimed she didn't really want, and would often then throw them away. She was the youngest of three sisters, and knew that her eldest sister had left home because of having suffered sexual abuse by their father. She claimed she had not been abused herself, and had what she termed, an 'on-off' relationship with both parents. Everything about her presentation was consistently ambivalent. She took a great deal of care over her makeup, yet said she tried to wear clothes that would make her look less attractive. One art therapy session, she titled her painting, 'sexuality'.

1. She had started by making a pencil outline of a naked female.
2. She had then reinforced that outline with black paint, painting a box around the head.
3. She had then clothed the body.
4. Finally scribbling over the outline very intensively, almost concealing parts of the image entirely.

Lee started by saying she would like to explore her picture, and when the group acknowledged this, she immediately followed this comment with the fact that she had no idea what the picture was about and that it was just a mess. Another member asked her why she had scribbled all over it, and Lee answered, 'I don't know, I just felt confused, that's what the picture is, it's just my confusion on paper'. When invited to begin to freely associate to the image, her answers became more and more muddled, until another member finally, said, 'I'm more confused than you now!'

The art therapist was at this point considering various possibilities. Confusion is often used as an unconscious defence against perceiving the reality of a situation, the subject feels too muddled to think, and therefore is protected from painful thoughts. This process can be observed in art therapy. Lee had not started out painting in a disorderly way, she had actively (although without conscious thought) attacked her image at a certain stage, the resulting picture looking indeed very confused. So what might Lee have been needing to protect herself from facing? Similarly, the scribbling was being verbally described by the woman as muddle. A very harmless word, with no violence attached to it. But the art therapist, having observed the process, had seen the actively destructive way in which the body had been attacked. Somehow Lee's perception had undergone a change from the point of doing the scribbling to the point of rather helplessly feeling 'muddled'.

These points are interesting when we reflect on the social expectations placed upon women with regards to their expression of anger. Women are socialised to be 'need-meeters' and this by definition implies that their own desires become subservient to others. Even in the most liberated of women this runs very deep and is compounded by the feeling that to a certain extent being sensitive to others needs is in fact a more humane way to relate to each other. The problem develops when those people's needs and wishes are not responded to with a corresponding degree of sensitivity. Underlying this is the threat of rejections, both personally and as a woman rejecting her assigned role. These issues have a direct bearing on the difficulty so many women have in expressing their anger. The suppression and distortion of this emotion goes hand in hand with the loss also of their power and vitality. We see again and again the destructive results of impotent rage as women maintain the splits, which are socially reinforced all around us, between the outer contained and containing self and the inner mess.

So with some of these reflections in mind, the therapist asked Lee to retrace the process of making her picture. Lee said she had started with the body outline, (which at first she professed was not her own), but hadn't liked the appearance of the pencil outline because it seemed too 'weak'. She had therefore strengthened it with the black paint. Another group member asked what the relevance was of the title 'sexuality'. Lee answered 'You've got to be tough, if you're seen as weak, you're easy prey'.

Now this comment had many dimensions to it. Lee worked in a high-pressure industry, where survival of the fittest was the rule. She may have on another level been referring to her need to protect herself sexually both in the world, as a reality and within her family, where her sister had been 'easy prey'. Psychologically, she was describing clearly her own need for her outer defenses to protect her very vulnerable inner self.

Lee continued to say that once she had painted the stark black outline over the original pencil line, it stood out too much and she had wanted to cover it up. She had memories of children's comics where she could cut out dresses and attach them to a picture of a young girl. She felt upset by these memories as if they represented a time of innocence before she had to deal with the anguish of having an adult woman's body. She went on to describe a feeling of panic when she had painted clothes on the body, heightening her awareness of her own wish to remain covered up. 'It's as if the fact that she was a female body means she's available'.

The therapist suggested that she was not only conveying something of the shame she experiences about her body but also her feeling of extreme vulnerability. This again needed to be recognised both on the psychological level, one in which Lee had not secured firm enough self-boundaries to maintain an ongoing sense of bodily integrity but simultaneously, she was reflecting real concerns which would have been shortsighted to only interpret on a personal level. She was also conveying also her sense of guilt for attracting sexual attention.

Lee said that the box around her head was to separate it from the rest of her revolting body. She was describing her attempts to create a division between what she thought of as her true self located from the neck up and her body which she wanted to disown. The final scribbling over the body had been a reaction to seeing her female shape which she despised. She was able to recognise the reality in the violent attack she had made on the picture, and the process of falsifying her own experience. The attack was linked to her repeated forms of self-harm and she closely linked it here with a feeling of guilt.

The guilt concerned many aspects of her life. Lee would regularly have to go to casualty departments to have her arms sutured, and was aware that this process demonstrated a form of concrete caring. It is interesting that this process demonstrated a form of concrete caring. It is interesting that so many women express their distress through this particular form of behaviour, which often results, as it did for Lee, in an immediate turnabout from one role to the opposite. It was as if Lee had not found ways of feeling cared about enough, and particularly at the threat of any separation or loss, she would find the need to have someone physically attending to her. Apart from Lee's own personal history, the frequency of this scenario does suggest that for large numbers of women, being taken care of rather than being the care-taker is highly problematic.

Lee's violent behaviour toward her own body involved a complicated number of issues. As with many women who self-mutilate, one of the precipitants she discovered was to increase a sense of aliveness, at points where she felt dead or empty. This important discovery came about through a series of art therapy sessions in which she was able to recognise a significant pattern which had previously remained unconscious to her. A number of her paintings would begin with energy and enthusiasm to communicate what was on her mind. Then at some point during the process, Lee would regularly find a loss of interest in her own work and ideas and the painting would similarly suffer. This would inevitably be followed by an attack on the image, often destroying the originally intended work altogether. By careful processing of this over a period of time, Lee was able to recognise that her initial wish to work, which entailed bearing a hope that there would be someone (the therapist or the group) there to communicate to, would regularly be thwarted by an internal voice which would tell her that no-one would really be interested in what she had to show. This was a reflection of her internalised perception of a rejecting mother whom she felt had been unable to adequately be available for her. In response to this message which she was now giving to herself, she would give up despairingly. This would be followed by an expression of her rage at the perceived abandonment.

Her destructiveness therefore was partially aiming to work as an anti-depressant. It also served to punish her for her neediness in the face of an absent other. She was able to regularly mutilate herself, (and one could consider her violent bingeing and vomiting also as forms of self abuse), partly because of the extent to which she was dissociated from ownership of her body. Her body was just a thing, 'flesh hanging up in a butchers shop' she had once described it as. Her body had not been fully incorporated into her self-image, or rather was regularly being disowned. Not only was her body the confused and hated combined image of herself and her mother, but she carried, as do so many of these women, many of their own mother's experiences of self loathing, devaluing and shame.

Not all of these experiences belong to the individual's psychopathology. Women are shamed into examining their bodies for excess hair, cellulite, stretch marks, sagging breasts and much more. The body is felt to be the guilty party. It causes men to lose control, it forces an awareness of dependency needs and creates hunger, it longs to be held when there is no one there and it can be blamed for feelings of worthlessness.

'Just because it wasn't me that my Dad abused, nobody thinks I've got any reason to hate my body', she cried in the art therapy session. Lee was struggling with a range of personal and social issues, in her battle to befriend her own body. She, similarly to Ann, had to wrestle with her internalised images of what it was to be a woman. And that had obviously been shaped not only through her own personal history, but, as for all women through the history of Womanhood.

REFERENCES

Dana, M. & Lawrence, M.(1988) *A New Understanding of Bulimia.* Grafton Books, London.

Eichenbaum, L. & Orbach, S. (1985) *Understanding Women.* Penguin Books, Harmondsworth.

Fox, J. (1987) *The Essential Moreno.* Springer Publishing Co., New York, USA.

Woodman, M. (1985) *The Pregnant Virgin.* Inner City Books, Toronto, USA

CHAPTER 10

Using the Metaphor of Compulsive Eating in Groups

Sheila Ritchie

Groups for women with a compulsive eating problem have been popular at the Women's Therapy Centre almost since its beginning. Many women who come have read 'Fat is a Feminist Issue', Orbach (1978) finding that its powerful message gives a voice to their feelings. What often resonantes is the recognition that the roots of their compulsive eating problem lie in how they have been socialised as women. Many identify as women who put others needs before their own, who do not feel entitled to take for themselves for fear of being seen as greedy or too demanding, many feel that they should not take up too much space in the world.

Some acknowledgement of the problem comes as a relief, often after repeated attempts to get help. Unfortunately, compulsive eating does not tend to be taken seriously, often overshadowed by anorexia or bulimia which can bring more medical complications. Women who then present with such a problem are often dismissed or told to go on a diet. For a woman who knows the ins and outs of just about any diet available this suggestion does nothing but accentuate her feeling that she is not entitled to help for her problems: she should take up even less space, restrict herself.

The Women's Therapy Centre offers a range of individual and group psychotherapy. Groups for women with a compulsive eating problem are offered on a brief (10 or 12 weeks) or longer term (one or two years) basis. For the purposes of this paper examples have been chosen from work in the brief groups by Clare Brennan and Sheila Ritchie.

WHAT THE GROUPS OFFER

The compulsive eating groups give each woman the opportunity to explore her relationship with food and discover why she has learnt to respond to her feelings with food rather than express them in some other way. Through her work in the group the aim is that she can begin to shift her dependence on her compulsive eating and explore how she might get her needs met through relationships with other people.

The groups are run analytically. This is made clear to the women at assessment and explained in terms of helping them make connections between what has happened to them in the past and how this has affected their current functioning and relationships. Group rules are explained such as a commitment to attend all sessions until the end of the group and not to meet group members outside of the group sessions.

It is hoped that at the end of the brief group the women will continue to find some other psychotherapy to continue working on the issues which the food masks. Help is offered to the women in finding further help from within or outside the Women's Therapy Centre, if requested.

The approach used by the therapists is to use the metaphor of the eating problem itself wherever possible in their interventions. The group gives the women an experience of a boundary; a clear beginning and an end. They are encouraged to express both their satisfaction and disappointment about their experience of being in the group. This has been found to be an effective way of helping each woman gain an insight into her problem and a way of helping her see that 'good' and 'bad' feelings can exist together.

Below is a description of some of the common themes of compulsive eating and illustrations of how they have emerged in brief groups.

HOW THE HUNGER IS ACKNOWLEDGED

The compulsive eater is out of touch with her hunger. Her eating keeps at bay the painful and dangerous feeling of emptiness and hunger: having to face the longings in her life. She finds it difficult to believe that she could ever get them met.

During one group session early on in the group's life the therapist's stomach rumbled. A series of very powerful feelings were evoked by this: one woman was angry that the hunger was so blatantly brought into the room, as if the therapist had done it on purpose. The display of hunger reminded her of the amount of time she spends trying to hide or pack down her own feelings with food and of her longing to be able to recognise her own needs, symbolised by her hunger.

Another woman talked about her feat that if the therapist were hungry, she would then have to feed her, just as she had felt she had had to look after her mother. Did it mean that she was not substantial enough – if she were empty, what could she possibly have to offer?

HOW THE SPACE GETS FILLED IN THE SESSION

For the woman who is a compulsive eater any space must be filled with food. If she is not eating she will be thinking about food, planning what she might eat. A meal is not enough, she will continue to pick at food or binge. Each mouthful becomes indistinguishable from another. She will often eat to the point where she cannot physically move, packing down her feelings until they are no more than a blur.

In a group it is common that there is very little silence. Often the space needs to be filled with words, a bit like a binge, continually moving on to the next point, not leaving any time to digest what is said or think about what it means. Thought often goes away from the present to the next 'meal', 'What will I do after the group?' or 'What will I do after the group has finished?' rather than 'What might I do during the group time?'. Silence becomes dangerous because it is in the emptiness that the painful feelings which seem so unmanageable are present.

Often the lack of direction in an analytic group feels particularly difficult for this group of women. They may try to find a way of dividing the time up fairly, or picking a theme to discuss, often focussing on food or diets, rather than allow the freedom to look at what may arise in the space in the group. The attempt at structuring can be used as a way of avoiding feelings like competition or envy and can be seen as an expression of a desire for some external control, like a diet.

THE SWING BETWEEN FAT AND THIN

It is very common to hear women who are compulsive eaters say 'If only I were thin I wouldn't have these problems' as if magically the awful feelings they have about themselves would disappear. They would be like the thin women in the television ads – competent, carefree, popular, sexually attractive. Different personalities and feelings are attributed to fat and thin people.

On further investigation it becomes clear that there is an ambivalence about being thin. Women will talk about times when they have been on diets and felt as though they could take control of their lives by controlling their bodies. However, 'thin' then takes on the meaning of being vulnerable and insubstantial or sexual and exposed so they put on weight again using (unconsciously) the fat as protection against these feelings.

Women in the groups are of varied size. There is usually quite a split between those who are thin and fat. The presence of thin women remind the fat women of their longing to be thin. When they have to face this in the room it is more difficult to sustain the belief that, 'If I were thin, things would be different'. This can leave the thin women in the group in a difficult position as if they are not entitled to their place in the group.

By contrast the fat women in the group may represent for the thin women their fear of taking up more space or the fear of being out of control with food. Seeing the other helps each woman reown the other part of herself so that she can begin to see that she is not either one or the other. In the same body she can be both strong and vulnerable, dependent and independent, whatever her individual meanings of fat and thin.

When a few women were absent from one group session there was a feeling of panic when one woman noticed that the larger women were on one side of the room and the smaller women (including the therapists) on the other. She talked of seeing the group as a boat which felt as if it were rocking and might capsize. This was at a stage of the group when the group members were beginning to experience the range of difficult feelings which they had been using food to avoid. The change felt threatening and the shift in feelings felt difficult to balance.

JUST ANOTHER SLIMMING CLUB?
However much group members realise that the group is not like a slimming club where the aim is to lose weight it is difficult for them not to judge the success of the group in these terms.

As some begin to experience their feelings in the group their eating patterns may begin to change and they can stop eating compulsively. They may then lose weight whilst at the same time learning to eat what they would like when they are hungry rather than having to resort to restricting themselves by going on a diet. For others there is the disappointment that they may continue to put on weight as the feelings triggered in the group will continue to be dealt with by food outside of the group. This can sometimes make the group seem like just another diet which has failed.

At the beginning of the group there is the longing to be told what to do, to have exercises structured, or to be given advice. This can be seen as the longing for some control which comes from outside. The aim is for the women to begin to find this sense of control for herself by developing an increased sense of her own self and her needs.

RELATIONSHIP WITH MOTHER

A need to depend on food rather than relationships to meet emotional needs often stems from the early mother-daughter relationship in the context of a society where women are socialised to be caretakers rather than have their own needs met. The girl identifies with a mother who does not get her own needs met. The mother identifies with her daughter as someone who has more opportunities to get her needs met and this puts her in touch with her own unmet needs. Unconsciously this can mean that the daughter gets the message that she must meet her mother's needs and be like her and comes to fear the isolation of being different from her mother.

It is not surprising that it is food that a woman turns to to comfort herself. She can go to the fridge and have a 24 hour supply of food but in relationships with others has to face the disappointments, the frustrations of waiting to have ner needs met or the fear that they may not be met at all.

Coming to the Women's Therapy Centre for therapy is particularly evocative for all women. There is often the hope that the centre will be the perfect mother, providing what is needed, a total understanding. Each woman has to face the painful disappointment and frustration when she realises that there is a limited amount on offer.

In the group the therapist(s) may come to represent the mother. Some women will relate to the therapist in a rejecting, angry way right from the start, not able to believe in the possibility that she may be able to get something from her. The therapist is seen as useless. She only offers 12 sessions. She can't be depended on therefore what's the point of trying to get anything from her. This anger can mask the intense feelings of longing and fear and uncertainty of having to wait between sessions, wondering whether there will ever be enough.

Sometimes the group members will refer to the group as a self help group, not wanting to acknowledge the role of the therapists, thereby denying the difference between therapist and group members and the feelings of dependence that can arise. There is also a tendency for similarities between the women to be highlighted so that differences do not have to be tolerated. The therapists are often seen as not having a compulsive eating problem, so how could they possibly understand what they might be feeling. Often the fear is that if their own difference or individuality were expressed in the group then the support they so desperately want would be destroyed. This makes it particularly important to explicitly deal with all differences in the group such as race, sexuality and age as well as differences about fat and thin. This will then better equip the women to distinguish between the range of different feelings inside themselves.

Co-leaders in groups, whatever their gender, can come to represent the parental couple. The group is likely to attempt to split one into the 'good' parent and one into the 'bad'. In one group of compulsive eaters, however, the group members seemed to be unable to distinguish between the two therapists, who in reality were quite different in appearance, age and style of working. The group members mixed up the names, forgot which therapist said what. The group members seemed to be treating the therapists as if their relationship mirrored their own difficult undifferentiated relationship with their own mother.

COMPLIANCE OR DEFIANCE?

Compulsive eating can be seen as both a compliance with and a defiance against the social expectations on women, the compliance in keeping feelings in and putting other's needs first, the defiance is not conforming to society's pressures to be thin. The women are often more in touch with their compliance, having to be a good girl rather than with their defiance.

Whilst the rules of the group are made clear i.e. no meeting the other group members outside the session, there can be a particular defiance about these rules in the group, which can come to symbolise society's expectations on women. In one group there was reluctance to stick to the time limit of the group. Women arrived earlier and earlier each week until there was a sub group meeting before the actual session began. The difficult feelings like anger were being expressed by women staying away or coming late or were talked about in the therapist's absence. By offering a firm boundary the women are more likely to begin to feel that their feelings can be managed.

WHERE DO MEN FIT IN?
The women have all chosen to be in a women only group. There is a high expectation that at last they will find someone who will understand. This is undoubtedly the case that in finding their experience mirrored by the other women they can feel less isolated and feel a deep emotional support. For many whose eating problem masks an experience of sexual or other abuse from men, it is clearly very important for them to be able to explore their feelings about this in the absence of men.

This intense closeness creates a safety which the women are reluctant to give up. This then makes it very difficult and painful for any feelings of difference or anger or competition to be expressed. The fear is that if difference is expressed the closeness will be destroyed.

In their lives outside the group the women can often allow men to carry these difficult feelings like anger and competition whilst men can allow women to carry the nurturing feelings. A woman only group gives an opportunity for these feelings to be reowned or reclaimed.

The power of the metaphor of food is clear for all women. Providing the opportunity for a woman to work on her relationship to food in a group context with other women can help break down the feeling of isolation she feels in having learnt to 'feed' herself. Instead of looking in the mirror or stepping on the scales to find out how she is feeling she can begin to trust that she may be able to take in nurturing from others and allow her own feelings to be acknowledged and responded to by both herself and others. She can begin to feel entitled to her place in the world.

ACKNOWLEDGEMENTS
I should like to acknowledge the women in the groups from whom we continue to learn so much, Clare Brennan, and the supervision group led by Sheila Ernst who keeps the boundary for us. Also Susie Orbach for her useful ideas about understanding women with eating problems.

REFERENCES
Orbach. S. (1978) *Fat is a Feminist Issue*

SEXUAL EXPERIENCES

CHAPTER 11

Eating Patterns and Unwanted Sexual Experiences

Rachel Calam & Peter Slade

There is an increasing debate in the literature concerning the extent to which unwanted sexual experiences may play some part in the aetiology of eating disorders. While most reports generally look at presence or absence of abuse, it may be that specific types of experience are of particular significance, or may have a particularly damaging effect. This chapter describes two studies of women in therapy for an eating disorder, and compares their responses to a Sexual Events Questionnaire (SEQ) to those obtained from women in therapy for mood disorder, and to women with no known history of eating disorder. Particular categories of sexual experience appeared to be of importance in the eating disorder groups. In particular, sexual experience with a close male relative was reported more frequently. The chapter discusses the ways in which unwanted sexual experiences may contribute to the development of an eating disorder.

There has been some debate in the literature recently over the question of whether women who have experienced sexual abuse or unwanted sexual experiences of some kind may be more likely to develop difficulties associated with eating. Some studies appear to indicate the possibility of a link between unwanted sexual experience and the later development of an eating disorder (Abraham & Beumont, 1982; Oppenheimer et al., 1985; Palmer et al., 1990).

However a study by Lacey, (1990) has not provided support for this hypothesis.

Some studies of non-clinic women (Calam & Slade, 1987; Beckman & Burns, 1990) have indicated that unwanted sexual experience may be associated with the development of problems associated with eating, as measured by self-report questionnaire, but other studies (Finn et al., 1986) have not supported this association. These authors have suggested that rather than tapping a real association between eating difficulties and unwanted sexual experience, what is happening is that both occur with such high rates in the female population as a whole and so there is a high probability that many women will have experienced both. Therefore, the evidence for a link is not clear.

For those women who have experienced unwanted sexual advances, the link is sometimes plain. Calam and Slade (1989) reported the perceptions of a group of women who had experienced a range of unwanted sexual encounters and who drew clear links between these and their subsequent development of a full-blown eating disorder. A common theme was that these women had lost control of their lives in some sense following the unwanted experience and the eating disorder permitted them some sense of regained control. Some women reported a desire to alter their body shape in order to avoid further sexual approaches. Others talked about their feelings of guilt, disgust, and self-hatred and said that their binge eating and vomiting in some sense formed a punishment for what they had experienced. Some of these women clearly thought that they had brought the abuse upon themselves. Others talked of parallels between their appetite for food and their appetite for sex. For these women gaining control of the appetite meant taking control of their sexual urges as well. A particularly striking feature for most of the women was that the unwanted sexual experience had often taken place at the time of other major problems and upheavals in their lives. Looking at these women's comments it is possible to draw up models of the ways in which unwanted sexual experience might lead to eating disorder. A rather straightforward model is presented in Figure 1.

In this linear model, the experience of abuse or other unwanted sexual experience leads to dissatisfaction with one's self and body, leading in turn to a desire to alter the body in some way and hence to dieting and subsequently to eating disorder. However Calam

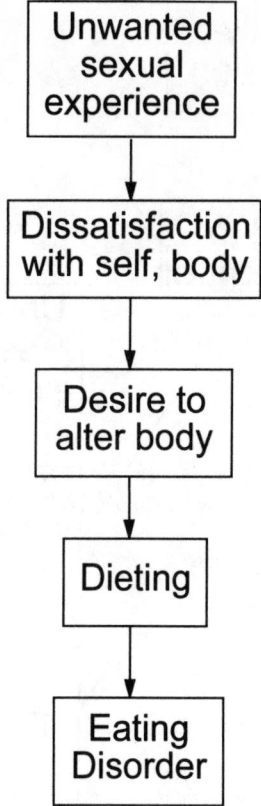

Figure 1 *A linear model for the translation of the experience of abuse into an eating disorder*

and Slade hypothesized that intrafamilial abuse might be associated specifically with anorexic symptomatology as self-starvation might act as a form of punishment toward an abusing parent or a parent who had failed to protect the woman from abuse from another family member. In this model (see Figure 2) some aspect of family interaction would make the individual more prone to abuse and also fuel a need to attain control over the family situation. In this setting, a change in eating patterns might become functional as a means of attaining control and hence lead on to the development of an eating disorder.

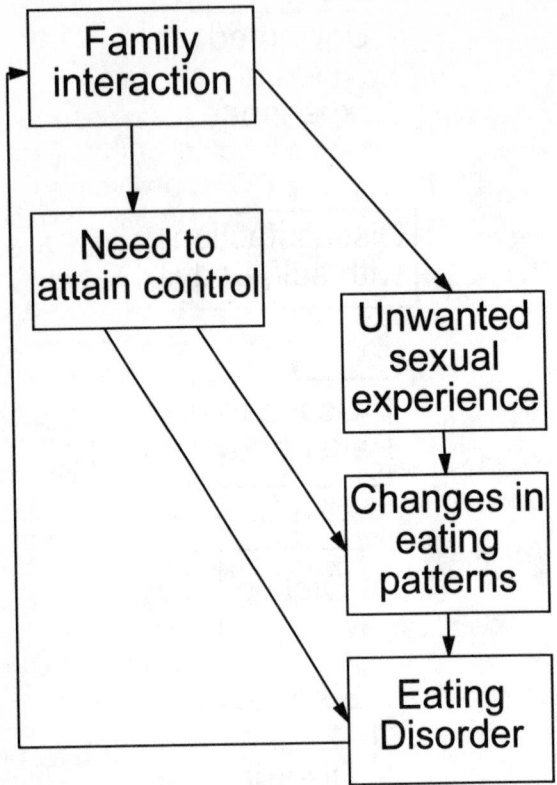

Figure 2 *A circular hypothesis for the relationship between the experience of abuse and eating disorders*

'SEXUAL EVENTS' SURVEY

To assess the extent to which unwanted sexual experience might contribute to the development of eating disorder we studied 49 women in therapy for eating disorders and a group of 60 female undergraduate students. All women completed a Sexual Events Questionnaire (SEQ) which asks about various sexual experiences, the age at which they occurred, and their impact on the respondent at the time. Using chi-square analysis, we found that women with eating disorders were significantly more likely to report having been upset by having someone expose their genitals to them (36% vs. 16%), more likely to have experienced forced sexual intercourse (30% vs. 15%), and more likely to have had a sexual experience with an authority figure (16% vs.

3%). They were also more likely to have had a sexual experience with a close male relative (20% vs. 5%). There was no difference between women with anorectic or bulimic symptoms.

In a second study in North America we compared a group of 37 eating disordered women with a group of 20 women with mood disorders attending a clinic. Again, it was found that the women with eating disorders were more likely to have been upset by having someone expose their genitals to them (32% vs. 5%). The women in the eating disorder group were also more likely to have had sexual contact with a close male relative (27% vs. 5%).

Overall the clinic groups reported more experiences of forced intercourse (30%, UK, 26%, USA) than did the students (15%) and higher incidence of actual or attempted rape (16%, UK, 14%, USA, 7%, students). The mood disorder patients reported a similar frequency of sexual contact with a close male relative to that reported by the students.

The data reported here would seem to indicate that propensity to report specific sexual experiences notably exposure, forced intercourse, sexual contact with an authority figure and sexual contact with a close male relative is more likely in women with eating disorders than those without. Moreover it would appear that it is particularly the experience of unwanted exposure and the experience of sexual contact with a close male relative which distinguishes women with eating disorder from women with mood disorder. Hence, although it might be anticipated that sexual contact within the family might have a globally disturbing and upsetting effect upon the individual, this did not appear to be the case. The women in the mood disorder sample were reporting rates of intrafamilial experience no higher than the comparison group. This might lead to the conclusion that there is something specific about contact within the family that might give rise to an eating disorder.

Clearly there are difficulties in interpreting data of this kind. The data are retrospective accounts given by questionnaire. With respect to exposure for example it may be that the women with eating disorder have a high level of sensitivity to any kind of exposure, so that which might be quite tolerable for a woman whose body image is not disturbed may be rated as distressing by a woman for whom bodily appearance and sexuality are of themselves extremely disturbing. It is also important to note that Calam and Slade's

hypothesis that intrafamilial abuse might lead specifically to anorexic symptomatology is simply not held up by the data. This
might lead to more general hypotheses about the effects of abuse
within the family. Hence for some women with anorexic symptomatology it may be that their eating disorder has become functional in
'turning off' the abuse while for others their bulimia might reflect
an overall sense of disturbance and distress over the use that has
been made of their bodies which might lead to very different
hypotheses about loss of control and the subsequent development
of bulimic symptomatology. Hence it may be the case that while
giving a message to the family about the abuse has some part to
play in the symptomatology it is not the whole of the picture.
Indeed in order for an eating disorder to develop it is probable that
a whole range of setting conditions are necessary (Slade, 1982).

It may be most appropriate to think of abuse or unwanted
sexual experience of some kind as one of a number of possible
setting conditions contributing to the overall development of the
eating disorder. Figure 3 presents a model which offers hypotheses
about some of the processes which may be involved in the development of an eating disorder where abuse or unwanted sexual experience is present.

The unwanted sexual experience is seen as leading to several
things: to a need to establish control over the environment; to
emotional change within the individual and also to changes in
eating patterns. Research on children who report sexual abuse very
frequently indicates that their eating patterns may change at least
in the short term and food refusal may be common (Peters, 1976).
Each of these factors will interact with personality factors of the
kind that Slade (1982) describes and may also have some effect
upon interaction within the family. As mentioned earlier the women
who we have interviewed report that there are often other problems
or major changes and upheavals going on in their lives at the
particular time that the unwanted experience took place and it may
be that, within the setting conditions that these help to create, the
change in eating patterns becomes functional. This helps the woman
to feel in control of things and may simultaneously have some
impact upon the family. In the case of intrafamilial abuse this may
be a particularly important factor, but for other women who have
had other experiences this may not be the case. Once established
the eating disorder leads to a change in the nature of other

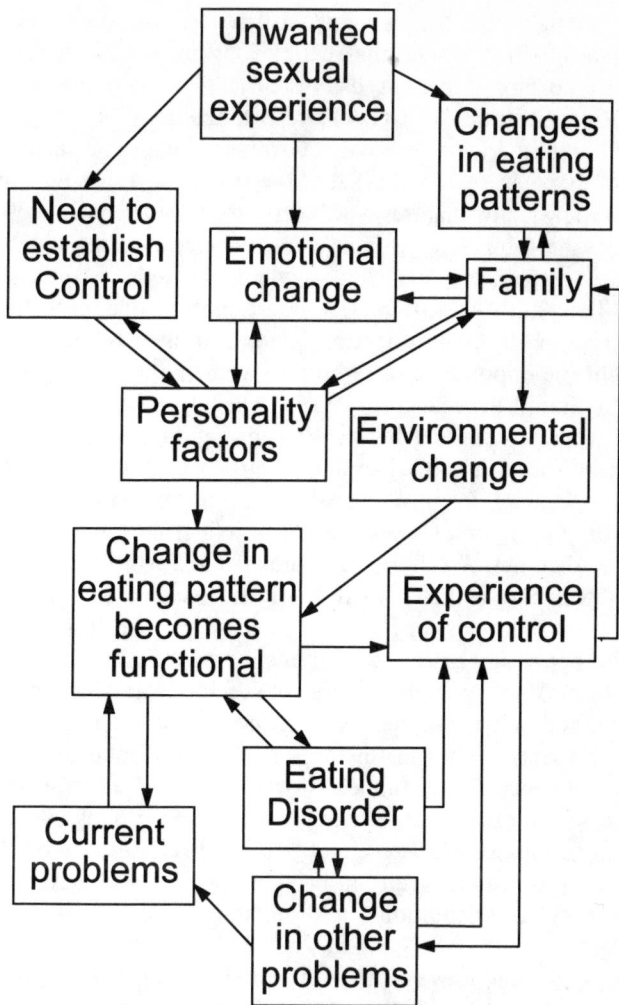

Figure 3 *A final model to explain relationships between unwanted sexual experience and eating disorders*

problems and may serve to make these seem less important. Hence it is possible to hypothesize that unwanted sexual experience may contribute to the development of an eating disorder in some extremely important way without being the sole factor accounting for it.

One particularly striking paper arising from a small study by Williams (1988) indicates that eating may indeed be difficult for women who have experienced abuse. Williams used the SEQ and the Eating Attitudes Test (EAT) with a group of 21 women who were attending Incest Survivors Groups. She found surprisingly high levels of scores on the EAT, the mean score for the women being 34.1, which compares with norms for female controls of 15.4. Further, she found that women who reported a larger number of unwanted experiences also had significantly higher scores on the EAT. This study is particularly interesting as it approaches the area from a different direction, and also because it serves to highlight the importance of talking to women about other areas of their life than the specific problem for which they were referred.

The women attending for therapy for eating disorders in Liverpool have found it helpful to have their sexual histories addressed and it is evident from Williams' survey of the women in Incest Survivors Groups that several could benefit from therapy for their eating difficulties. We hope very much that further patient series studies will be conducted as it is still not clear from the data to what extent links exist or how specific these may be. In particular it would appear important to conduct hypothesis-led research in order to look with a higher degree of specificity at what the nature of links between unwanted experience and eating patterns might be. At present, studies in this area address a number of different questions. One, for example, is whether rates of reporting of specific sexual experiences are higher in certain groups. Another is whether certain experiences are of particular relevance to particular groups. An overall difficulty in bringing the studies together lies in the variety of definitions and methodologies used in data collection.

It is very clear however that, as Palmer et al. (1990) conclude, women in therapy need the opportunity to talk about their sexual experiences and to be helped to explore the extent to which experiences which they have had may be affecting their current behaviour and emotional state. We have found that a questionnaire approach can be a relatively gentle and non-threatening way of approaching questions in this very difficult area and many women have said that they are very pleased to be able to talk about their experiences.

ACKNOWLEDGEMENTS
The North American study was conducted at BASH, St. Louis. The authors would like to thank Dr. Felix Larocca, Director of BASH, and Vicki Jones, Senior Research Assistant for making available the preliminary BASH data on the SEQ.

REFERENCES
Abraham, S. & Beumont, P.J.V. (1982) Varieties of psychosexual experience in patients with anorexia nervosa. *International Journal of Eating Disorders*, 1: 10–19.

Beckman, K.A. & Burns, G.L. (1990) Relation of sexual abuse and bulimia in college women. *International Journal of Eating Disorders*, 9: 487–492.

Calam, R.M. & Slade, P.D. (1987) Eating problems and sexual experience: some relationships. *British Review of Bulimia and Anorexia Nervosa*, 2: 37–43.

Calam, R.M. & Slade, P.D. (1989) Sexual experience and eating problems in female undergraduates. *International Journal of Eating Disorders*, 8: 391–397.

Finn, S.E., Hartman, M., Leon, G.R. & Lawson, L. (1986) Eating disorders and sexual abuse: lack of confirmation for a clinical hypothesis. *International Journal of Eating Disorders*, 5: 1051-1060.

Lacey, J.H., (1990) Incest, incestuous fantasy and indecency: A clinical catchment area study of normal-weight bulimic women. *British Journal of Psychiatry*, 157: 399–403.

Oppenheimer, R., Howells, K., Palmer, R.L. & Chaloner, D.A. (1985) Adverse sexual experiences in childhood and clinical eating disorder: a preliminary description. *Journal of Psychiatric Research*, 19: 357–361.

Palmer, R.L., Oppenheimer, R., Dignon, A., Chaloner, D.A. & Howells, K. (1990) Childhood sexual experiences with adults reported by women with eating disorders: an extended series. *British Journal of Psychiatry*, 156: 699–703.

Peters, J.J. (1976) Children who are victims of sexual assault and the psychology of offenders. *American Journal of Psychotherapy*, 30: 398–421.

Slade, P.D. (1982) Towards a functional analysis of anorexia nervosa and bulimia nervosa. *British Journal of Clinical Psychology*, 21: 67–79.

Williams, H. (1988) *An investigation into the relationship between eating disorders and sexual abuse in a group of survivors of sexual abuse.* Unpublished undergraduate project, Department of Psychology, University of Manchester.

CHAPTER 12

A Sexual Education Programme for Women with Eating Disorders

Ellie van Vreckem & Walter Vandereycken

Issues of being a grown up woman with a female identity and intimate sexual relationships, as well as issues like autonomy and self-definition are often addressed in anorexia and bulimia nervosa therapy programmes. In our own therapy centre we set up a sexual education group to create a stimulating and safe atmosphere in which women with eating disorders could communicate more freely about sexual themes. This chapter reports an evaluation of this group after two years.

Clinical experience and research have shown the important role of sexual problems and traumas in the development of anorexia nervosa and bulimia. Bearing this in mind we decided to experiment with a special sex-education programme for women with eating disorders. It began as purely educational group sessions, which provided more information for our very young patients and created a stimulating atmosphere to communicate more freely about sexual themes. Later on the sessions shifted to group meetings with more intimate and personal expressions of bodily experiences, sexual feelings and problems. Our in-patient unit of twenty women is divided into two groups, according to the level of sexual experience, the age and the treatment phase of each person. As 'warming up material' we use books and video films, which the groups are asked to read and watch one or two days before the meeting. The groups are conducted by a female psychologist and one of the female nurses.

Before we started the experiment we discussed our plans with the parents and partners of our patients. After some hesitation they were enthusiastic and collaborated actively. Some partners bought the book and read it together with our client.

The themes of the discussions are: falling in love; body experience and images; menstruation; sexuality; contraception and choice of partner. At the end of each session the group decides which one of six themes they would like to explore in the next session.

FEELINGS OF 'FALLING IN LOVE'

Each group member is asked to share with the group, as concretely as possible, her first 'love' experiences, feelings, disappointments, memories and fantasies.

The women can talk about some nice and tender feelings, but also about their disappointments, tensions and anxieties (such as secret feelings about some teacher or classmate). Particularly the impression of 'being out of control' when falling in love is very frightening for these women. Again and again they report their two extreme attitudes, being overwhelmed by others and by their own feelings or staying distant and unattainable. This is a very important issue to deal with in our treatment, because we are convinced that finding a position in-between is essential in building up one's individuality. After such experiences of 'weakness' women often start either an even more rigorous diet or a binge period in order to punish themselves, or others, through abusing their own body.

In the younger group girls talk for the first time about their amorous feelings and are ashamed but also surprised that they can enjoy talking about them. In the group composed of older women they react more with nostalgia, realising for themselves how much they have repressed their feelings and memories.

It is surprising how often the women have forgotten their first love experiences, or even forgotten the whole period of their young adolescence. The reactions of their parents were often most denigrating, ridiculing or over-controlling. In one case for instance the parents would demand to meet the new boyfriend immediately and pass endless comments upon his character and background etc. We systematically ask about the reactions of brothers and sisters to these romantic feelings. A general attitude amongst the women is to keep all their feelings secret from their brothers. The reactions of sisters is also often remembered as extreme: either positive and supporting or extremely jealous. We wonder if this is also a feeling of their own projections of jealousy onto others or their peers. We know that this mechanism is often found in families with eating disordered women: the outside world is considered dangerous and bad and therefore all negative feelings are placed outside the family.

In the group we try to create a pleasant atmosphere. Mostly these group sessions are the most relaxing of all, we laugh a lot about the funny feelings, forgotten fantasies or clumsy reactions.

BODY EXPERIENCES AND IMAGES

During these group sessions the 'mirror exercises' are discussed as well as memories about first body changes in puberty and reactions to it from parents, siblings and peers.

Coming from the body-orientated therapies, our mirror exercises are a focus of our treatment programme (Probst et al., 1990). The women carry out these 'mirror exercises' in the bathroom on the unit and they choose for themself the group member with whom they wish to do the exercises. Together they decide a time, often a quiet moment during the weekend. Dressed in a bathing suit and standing before a full size mirror they look at each other's bodies, commenting and expressing their feelings about their changing bodies. Taking into account the absence of an integrated body image, we encourage the women to focus upon different parts of their body as well as the body as a whole. Anorexics and bulimics are often fixed upon some specific part of their body.

These mirror exercises have several objectives, but the most important is the enhancement of formation of a stable, integrated, cohesive mental representation of one's own body. This is, as Krüger (1989) states, 'a core body image of what is inside and what is outside and a distinct sense of boundaries between the two'.

In our treatment we try to achieve this complex objective step by step and we believe that the mirror exercises constitute one of these steps. Instead of denying their real body we ask the women to clearly look at it – most of our clients report that they have not done this for months or even years. We ask them to verbalise their feelings to each other, to replace their critical eyes with loving ones and to focus upon the internal sensations and images. Anorexics and bulimics have a lack of internal evocative images of their body-self or their physiological self. They tend to rely upon external referents such as the reactions of others (Krüger 1989) or, even more often, their imagined reactions of others. By doing these exercises in pairs women can pay attention not only to their own internal work of building up body image, but also to their companions work in an intimate atmosphere. They can notice more easily the distortions and generalisations expressed by other women and thus realise their own distortions. It is also important that the atmosphere should be empathic and non-intrusive. In order to strengthen the evocation of internal body images in the art therapy sessions we ask the women to also draw the pictures of their body which they have in their own mind. Although this was developed as an evaluation method, we find it a useful a therapeutic tool.

Comments and warnings: The women do these exercises in the absence of a therapist, but this activity must not be isolated from the rest of the programme. Patients are expected to report their experiences back to the group sessions. We have noticed two major pitfalls:

1. *The choice of partner.* We encourage these exercise to be carried out once a week, with as many different group members as possible. When patients always select the same companion (perhaps because she is thinner) the reasons behind this must be explored in the group session.
2. *Feelings of rivalry and competition.* These issues are often enhanced, thus carrying out the exercise with various group members gives the women an opportunity to see all kinds of body shapes. In this way they help each other accept the differences of their bodies. Very often this is mentioned as the most positive aspect of mirror sessions.

In summary we should like to emphasise that these mirror sessions have to be considered as part of the total treatment programme and are linked firstly with the body oriented therapy and secondly with the group sessions on sexuality. Within this theme-session attention is sometimes given to the very frightening topic of masturbation. Masturbation as a way of discovering ones own body in a pleasant and loving way seems very difficult to grasp especially for the anorectic women. Women with bulimia are more familiar with it, but always seem to feel guilty and perhaps seek more painful sexual stimuli.

MENSTRUATION

We talk about the myths concerning menstruation, the influence of social and cultural factors on the experience of menarche and about menstruation as a symbol of female sexual maturation.

All too often we find deep rooted ideas such as that women who are menstruating are unclean, contaminated, sick, to be avoided and prohibited from sexual intercourse. All too often menstruation is also associated with pain, distress, tensions and irritability. In an interesting article O'Toole (1988) describes how she works around these issues in her art therapy sessions. In order to facilitate the expression of feelings and memories she uses expressive techniques (psychodrama, role playing) creative writing, journal keeping and guided fantasies to re-experience first menstruations. Painful memories and negative emotions have to be accepted and shared with the group. These are counterbalanced by exploring positive associations, by creating new rituals within the group. In our groups we create a ritual celebration of the return of menses each time it happens in treatment, the woman is warmly congratulated.

OTHER FORMS OF SEXUALITY

We use guided imagery to assist women in remembering past sexual experiences for instance from early sex play with peers, homosexual feelings or encounters which were traumatic or violent. Women are asked to discuss how they felt about their bodies and their eating behaviour at that time. If incest or some traumatic experience has occurred the women most often link this to the beginning of their eating problems and try to express these feelings in the group. These group sessions are the most painful, touching and intense of all. We always work very seriously with these revelations and try to integrate them into the other regular group psychotherapy sessions (thrice weekly) and/or in separate family sessions.

We also ask our clients to examine their present lives and to recognise self-destructive patterns or relationships where they were victimised. The effects of repeated victimisation are discussed, for instance how each experience deepens their distrust of other people and increases their feelings of loneliness and isolation (see also Kearney-Cooke, 1988).

It is remarkable how often group members want to speak about homosexual feelings, doubts and events, whilst being very reluctant to speak at the same time. These ideas of being 'not normal' or being homosexual appear very difficult to accept. The women often question themselves about their close friendships with other women and often need to be reassured.

CONTRACEPTION

Different forms and methods of contraception are discussed and demonstrated in the group. Each group member talks about her experiences, fears and doubts. This often turns out to be the most 'medical' session of all.

CHOICE OF PARTNER

In these group session the participants are asked to share the rational and irrational elements in their attraction to partners.

Which physical or personal qualities are important in order to feel some attraction? Is there a difference between sexual attraction and emotional closeness? How does this feel for each group member? How was it in the past and how is it now?

Mostly the women start to talk about long forgotten events and feelings. The conscious preference for distinguished, fair haired men in contrast to desperately falling in love with the opposite – mysterious dark haired ones is very usual. To us this is an opportunity for the women to get in touch with contradictory feelings, to wake up their curiosity about their own mystery and repressed longings for adventurous love.

During these sessions a remarkable transformation within the members takes place. They become more playful, vivid and fond of teasing, as if they feel released. Other longings can also be explored, the need to be admired or to participate in the admiration of others. Why do they so often fall in love with the 'play boy' which is experienced as very threatening. The need to nurture and to be nurtured is frequently mentioned as part of the attraction of a partner.

Very often anorexic girls with possessive mothers and/or fathers unconsciously choose possessive or even jealous partners. In this context the girls enrich their discussions with questions about fear of infidelity and abandonment, but also fear of boredom, control and lack of freedom and individuality within a relationship.

Finally the image of the father and/or brother can not be avoided. How much does the partner resemble or differ from the image of the father? Young girls as well as married women tell us about the funny, surprising or previously unnoticed details they like or dislike in their partners. We consider these group discussions as an opening of doors to a more personalised intimacy.

CONCLUSIONS

Taking into account the positive reactions of our clients and our own impressions, we are convinced that our sexual education programme stimulates the disclosure and discussion of sexual issues. Our impressions are that the women with anorexia nervosa seem to benefit more from these groups than the bulimic women, whose sexuality has to be more structured than liberated. The central theme for all of our clients is always the difficulty of handling growing intimacy with others without being overwhelmed by it. By recognising and accepting these feelings, particularly the contradictory ones, the women can begin to assert themselves in intimate relationships.

REFERENCES

Kearney-Cooke A. (1988) Group treatment of sexual abuse among women with eating disorders. *Women and Therapy*, 7: 5–21.

Krüger D.W. (1989) *Body self and psychological self*. New York, Brunner Mazel.

O'Toole C. (1988) Exploring female sexuality through expressive therapies, *The Arts in Psychotherapy*, 15: 109–117.

Probst M., Van Coppenholle H., Vandereycken W. (1990) Evaluating the body experience of patients with eating disorders through video-confrontation. In Doll-Tepper G. et al. (eds) *Adapted physical activity*. Berlin, Springer-Verlag.

Probst M., Van Coppenholle H., Vandereycken W., Meerman R. (1990) Zur evaluation der körperbild wharnehmung bei patienten mit anorexia nervosa. *Psychiatrische Praxis*, 17: 115–120.

WHAT ABOUT THE MEN?

CHAPTER 13

Self-help Groups for People with Eating Disorders: Is There a Place for Men?

Pat Hartley

This article looks at some of the issues surrounding the involvement of men in self-help groups for eating disordered patients, their relatives and friends. There is tentative evidence that the incidence of eating disorders in men is increasing. To deny access to male patients would be to discriminate unfairly against them. As support is offered to family and friends it would be equally unfair to exclude the male subgroup. Accepting males into a self-help group may increase the men's sensitivity to women's needs. It may also modify the female perception of male issues. Women are under some pressure to conform to society's expectations, but men may also have difficulty in meeting the high demands of today's competitive world. The changing role of women in society may lead the less secure male to question his own identity. The self-help group provides a safe forum for such issues to be explored. The presence of men in a self-help group may enable women to deal more confidently with men, within and outside the group. Many women clients are treated by male clinicians, male therapists may increase their own understanding of women's life experience by attending the groups. The aims of the self-help group include increasing awareness and understanding of eating disorders and it seems imperative that the knowledge and information members possess should be available to all, regardless of gender.

The acknowledgement by William Gull (1874) of the occasional occurrence in men, led to the term 'anorexia nervosa' being used in preference to 'anorexia hysteria' as hysteria was considered a uniquely female condition. More recent studies disclose an approximate ratio of eighteen female to one male sufferer. To deny access to self-help and support would be to discriminate unfairly against the male patient. Further, as there are relatively few cases in men, separate self-help groups are simply not feasible. Studies of younger patients with anorexia nervosa have shown a higher incidence in males than would be expected from the adult prevalence figures. (Fossen, Knibbs, Bryant-Waugh & Lask, 1986; Jacobs & Isaacs, 1986). Several useful studies have compared male and female patients, finding similar clinical features in both groups. (Vandereycken & Van den Broucke, 1984).

Although many interesting theoretical explanations have been postulated for the higher incidence of eating disorders in women, as yet none has been conclusive. It has been maintained that women are prey to greater cultural and societal pressures than men. Such pressures tend to find powerful expression through the media and focus not simply on the traditional role of women as carers and support systems but also on the ideal shape, size and appearance to which such carers should aspire. These messages frequently contain conflicting demands. A detailed discussion of these issues is beyond the scope of this paper but one media image is that the perfect wife must ensure that she provides only 'safe' foods for her husband who must be mindful of his cholesterol levels. Equally, as a mother, she must answer to her children's frequent requests for 'fast food'. At the same time, however, if she is to maintain her relationship with her partner and the admiration of her children, she must not eat any of these foods herself.

The media exploit men too within this process as even male products are frequently promoted through the inclusion of the ideal female with the ideal car which successful men are meant to possess. The notion that such pressures are confined to women may therefore be refuted by some men. In recent years expectations imposed on men have changed in focus. There is still great emphasis on strength and power in the male. Such strength is displayed in physical terms in films for example – the Rambo series – and the 'macho' image beloved by body-builders. Physical fitness in males can be achieved by exercise and diet. In addition, contemporary philosophy requires high levels of success in career terms, with, it may be suggested, little regard for success in personal relationships. Modern man, however, is also encouraged to find his mate. This final goal is to be sought by the same process by which all goals may be achieved – strength and power. There is much emphasis on the male as financial provider for his family but little in the way of the satisfier of their emotional needs. Women, responding to the media 'ideal' male, but at some level recognising their own emotional needs, would perhaps prefer some kind of 'combination model'. Such confusion may lead to internal conflict in both women and men. The more sensitive man, in the face of this conflict, may question his role in society and also his personal identity.

In the case of male patients some useful information about family relationships has been provided. Sreenivasan (1978) described a family background typical of his sample of male anorexics. 'The mothers, oversensitive and insecure, were partnered by men who project the cultural image of masculinity, including over-indulgence in alcohol. The parents as a whole were over-weight, but obesity was more noticeable in the fathers. The patients were relatively immature and obsessional, two being markedly obsessional. The families were skewed, with marital difficulties and overt hostility between fathers and patients on the one hand, and over-dependence between the mothers and patients on the other. The onset of severe calorie restriction followed real or feared obesity.' Perhaps men view eating disorders as one way of rebelling against society's image of the ideal male.

Of the five men seen within the Salford project, two had failed aspirations to a career in professional football, one is a policeman with fifteen years experience, one is a commercial artist and the fifth is unemployed. All describe very poor relationships with their fathers who in the case of those in employment, had chosen their careers for them. These fathers had reacted very negatively to both failure in the footballers and expressed dissatisfaction with his occupational role by the policeman. Interestingly, the artist and the unemployed patient had long ago severed all connection with their fathers and had made more progress towards recovery than the other three who were still very much involved with their original families, though all were married with children of their own.

One of the functions of the self-help group is to increase levels of understanding about eating disorders. As self-help groups embrace families and friends as well as sufferers, it would be inappropriate to exclude fathers, partners, brothers or friends. To do so would in fact impoverish the experience of female group members.

Much has been written about poor communication in eating disordered families. By providing a non-threatening environment, self-help groups can facilitate communication, providing a useful forum where women can increase the male's understanding of female needs but conversely gain more insight into the needs of men. Male partners, hearing from other women about the way they experience life in general and relationships in particular, may thus be able to understand and accept similar sentiments when expressed by their own female friends or partners. In this way change may be possible.

Many women attending self-help groups are receiving treatment from male clinicians. The presence of men in the self-help group may lead to a greater sense of trust in the male therapist and greater confidence in their own ability to deal with relationships with males, inside and outside the group. Conversely, male therapists may have much to learn from attending the self-help group where women feel free to express themselves honestly.

The precise incidence of sexual abuse in the history of the eating disordered client is as yet unknown. It is sufficiently well-documented to be seen as a serious factor in many cases. The safety of the self-help group where individuals are free to be themselves, would enable women who have been abused to develop some sense of trust in relationships with men in a setting where sexuality is not a predominant issue.

Where families attend self-help group meetings some discussion may focus on the role of parents. It is believed that parents act as role models for their offspring. In normal circumstances, children, even as adults, rarely gain the opportunity to comment on the type of parenting they receive. The self-help groups can provide this opportunity, allowing sons and daughters to explain how they perceive their own needs, which may or may not be met by parents. Equally, both mothers and fathers may express to clients the difficulties they experience as parents.

Many of those at self-help groups are from single-parent families. Where the single parents are mothers, the presence of fathers in the group extends the experience of the young person growing up in a predominantly female household. In addition, at the Salford group there are several fathers who come alone. Neither the sufferers nor their mothers have attended throughout a three-year period. In these cases, the presence of these men is crucial – not only for their daughters' sake but also for those female sufferers who may not personally have experienced such a sensitive and caring attitude in their own male contacts.

In conclusion, the aims of the self-help group include increasing awareness and understanding of eating disorders. The knowledge and expertise contributed by sufferers, families, friends and health professionals should be available to all, regardless of gender.

REFERENCES

Fossen A., Knibbs J., Bryant-Waugh R. & Lask B. (1986) Early onset anorexia nervosa. *Archives of Diseases in Childhood*, 62: 114–18.

Gull W.W. (1874) Anorexia nervosa (apepsia hysteria, anorexia hysteria). *Transactions of the Clinical Society*, London, 7: 22–8.

Jacobs B.W. & Isaacs S. (1986). Pre-pubertal anorexia nervosa: a retrospective controlled study. *Journal of Child Psychology and Psychiatry*, 27: 237–50.

Sreenivasan U. (1978) Anorexia nervosa in boys. *Canadian Psychiatric Association Journal*, 23: 159- 62.

Vandereycken W. & Van den Broucke S. (1984). Anorexia nervosa in males. *Acta Psychiatrica Scandinavica*, 70: 447–54.

CHAPTER 14

Anorexia Nervosa in Boys

Rachel Bryant-Waugh

The presentation of anorexia nervosa in boys and young adolescent males remains relatively poorly documented. A number of studies have suggested that in this younger age-group the male-female ratio is higher than in older adolescents and young adults presenting for treatment of anorexia nervosa. This chapter addresses this issue and poses three main questions:

Is 'anorexia nervosa' in these younger boys the same as in girls and older individuals?

Is the prognosis the same for boys with anorexia nervosa as it is for girls?

How might the apparently higher ratio of males in the younger age group be explained?

It is proposed that gender issues may be less central to the development of eating disorders in children than in older individuals. Clinical descriptions and observations will be used to illustrate some of the ideas put forward.

In our own retrospective study of the presentation, course and outcome of anorexia nervosa in children aged between 8 and 14 years (Fosson et al., 1987; Bryant-Waugh et al., 1988) we found an unusually high number of males. Thirteen (or 27%) of the 48 children included in our study were boys, including one set of male twins. This was of great interest to us, as the figure of 27% of a clinical population of subjects with anorexia nervosa being male, is very high compared to estimates of the percentage of males in older age at onset patients (that is, adolescents and young adults). The ratio of males to females is usually placed somewhere between 1 to 10 (9%) and 1 to 20 (5%) (Vandereycken & Van de Broucke, 1984; Hall et al., 1985). However, Jacobs & Isaacs (1986) found a similarly high percentage of males in their study of young anorexia nervosa patients: 6 (or 30%) of their series of 20 pre-pubertal anorexics were male. Hawley (1985) described a series of 21 anorexia nervosa patients under the age of 14 at onset, four (or 9%) of whom were boys, and Higgs et al.'s (1989) study included eight boys (or 30%) from a total of 27 cases of anorexia nervosa in subjects aged 8–16 years at onset. We became rather suspicious that these findings all related to British clinical populations, but Nielsen (1990) also identified a similarly elevated percentage of males in the younger age range in his epidemiological study of anorexia nervosa in Norway: in the 10–14 year age group around 20% of cases were boys. These figures of around 20–30% of young clinic populations being male, combined with a steady stream of referrals of boys to our own eating disorders clinic leads us to the conclusion that in children, males present for treatment of an eating disorder at a higher ratio to females than is the case in older patients. At least three questions arise from this, which will be addressed in turn.

IS 'ANOREXIA NERVOSA' IN THESE YOUNGER BOYS THE SAME AS IN GIRLS AND OLDER INDIVIDUALS?

It is generally agreed that anorexia nervosa can and does occur in men (Crisp & Burns, 1983). There are some obvious sex related differences in presentation, such as ammenorrhea being the manifestation of endocrine disturbance in females, but on the whole there appears to be little difference between the sexes in terms of the physical features of the disorder (Sterling & Segal, 1985). Weight loss, emaciation, hormonal changes and starvation related symptoms are found in both males and females. In children, the physical features are also similar in both sexes. It is more difficult to be certain that the psychopathology of the eating disorder are the same in both sexes. It seems generally agreed that both display the characteristic fear of fatness, refusal to maintain a normal weight, and rigidity in thinking. These features are also in our experience at the Hospital for Sick Children, found in younger patients of both sexes. The following case illustrates this.

> Matthew was an 8 year old pre-pubertal boy with a twelve month history of eating problems and reduced food intake. This had become pronounced over the month prior to referral. On examination he was found to be 80% of the appropriate weight for his height. He had not previously been overweight. He was engaging in excessive exercising and had started to spit out saliva because he was worried about swallowing extra fluid. He did not appear to be vomiting, bingeing or abusing laxatives at presentation. He displayed a marked fear of fat and was low in affect. He stated that he felt fat despite being very thin. He claimed that he did not want to eat, because he wanted to be an athlete (a runner), and so could not afford to allow himself to become fat. He showed an increasing interest in cooking and had taken to helping his mother with the preparation of meals. He was considered to fulfill DSM-III-R criteria for anorexia nervosa.

It has been suggested that male anorectics have a tendency towards homosexuality or that in general they show some disturbance in the development of their gender identity (Fichter & Daser, 1987). Males experiencing sexual role conflicts and gender concerns are thought by some to have an increased risk for the development of an eating disorder (Herzog et al., 1984). This view is by no means universally held – for example, Crisp and his colleagues claim that there is no evidence to suggest that male anorectics have a disturbed gender identity (Crisp et al., 1986). Clearly, this is a complex issue, and one that involves information that is very difficult to obtain reliably and objectively. In children, we do not consider this to be a particularly useful theory. The question of whether these younger boys have 'true' anorexia nervosa remains difficult to answer with absolute certainty. Some systematic investigation is urgently required to clarify the nature of the core psychopathology of younger patients of both sexes with anorexia nervosa, not just the boys. However, it is our clinical view that boys and girls can present with anorexia nervosa from around the age of eight upwards. The illness they develop is similar in both sexes, certainly in physical terms, as well as many core cognitive and behavioural components being shared. All the boys attending the clinic who receive a diagnosis of anorexia nervosa fulfill, in our view, DSM-III-R criteria (APA, 1987) as well as our own diagnostic checklist (Fosson et al., 1987). It is perhaps of interest to note (and possibly the cause of some of the diagnostic uncertainty around young male patients) that over the past five years or so we have been seeing a much wider range of types of eating disorder in boys attending our clinic. Whereas the majority of the girls have anorexia nervosa, and only relatively few some other type of disorder, a greater proportion of boys present with other disorders characterised by low weight and eating difficulties, which are clearly not anorexia nervosa. These other childhood eating disorders include what Higgs et al. (1989) have called 'food avoidance emotional disorder', or other highly selective eating patterns, usually involving only two or three different foods (see further Bryant-Waugh & Kaminski, 1993).

IS THE PROGNOSIS THE SAME FOR BOYS WITH ANOREXIA NERVOSA AS IT IS FOR GIRLS?

Opinions tend to vary in the literature about the prognosis for males with anorexia nervosa. Some authors have suggested that being male is in itself a poor prognostic indicator in anorexia nervosa (Kalucy et al., 1977). Others have found that outcome varies according to the presence or absence of specific background and clinical features to a similar extent in both sexes; for example, Hall et al. (1985) stated that outcome in the male anorexia nervosa patients in their study was comparable to female patients at a three year follow-up. Burns & Crisp (1985) have commented upon the 'remarkable similarity in outcome pattern' between males and females, but also found that whereas vomiting predicts poor outcome in females, it is associated with good outcome in males (Crisp et al., 1986). There has been little consistency in the reported findings of outcome in male anorexia nervosa patients in general. This may be partly due to the fact that most studies include relatively small numbers of males, so that it becomes difficult to identify clear prognostic indicators. In our own previous follow-up study (Bryant-Waugh et al., 1988) we found that boys and girls differed significantly on two outcome scores:

• as a group the boys obtained lower scores on the 'nutritional status' subscale of the revised Morgan-Russell Outcome Scales

(Morgan & Russell, 1975). This subscale is an assessment of eating behaviour, weight and sensitivity to weight at outcome.
- as a group the boys obtained lower scores on the 'psychosexual adjustment' subscale (Morgan & Russell, 1975).

The number of boys included in this study was again rather small, and it is simply not possible at this stage of our knowledge to make any definitive statements about potential differences in prognosis or outcome between boys and girls. Our clinical view is that boys we see show similar variation in outcome to the girls: some appear to make complete recoveries, others continue to experience some difficulty around weight or eating but are able to function reasonably well, whilst yet others develop another form of disorder, typically an obsessional or anxiety related disorder. Unfortunately a minority, as with the girls, continue to be caught up in a destructive eating disorder that is resistant to our efforts to help.

HOW MIGHT THE APPARENTLY HIGHER RATIO OF MALES IN THE
YOUNGER AGE GROUP BE EXPLAINED?

In our own thinking and clinical work with children with anorexia nervosa at Great Ormond Street, we have found Slade's (1982) model for understanding the emergence and maintenance of eating disorders extremely helpful. He views anorexia nervosa as an 'attempted adaptive strategy given the major setting conditions of the individual's current life situation' (Slade, 1982). Figure 1 represents a simplification of his model for the development of anorexia nervosa and highlights three main areas of relevance in trying to understand the onset of the eating disorder: individual vulnerability, background conditions and triggering factors.

Given that the end point – the eating disorder – is essentially similar in individuals of all ages (which we believe to be the case, although this does remain a matter of debate and one requiring proper investigation), we need to consider background conditions, individual vulnerabilities and triggering factors in the context of different ages or stages of development. It can be suggested that some of the more common background factors and precipitating factors that are often thought to play a significant role in the development of eating disorders in children are less sex specific that in older individuals. That is, the more commonly identified contributory factors include things like parental separation, a family move,

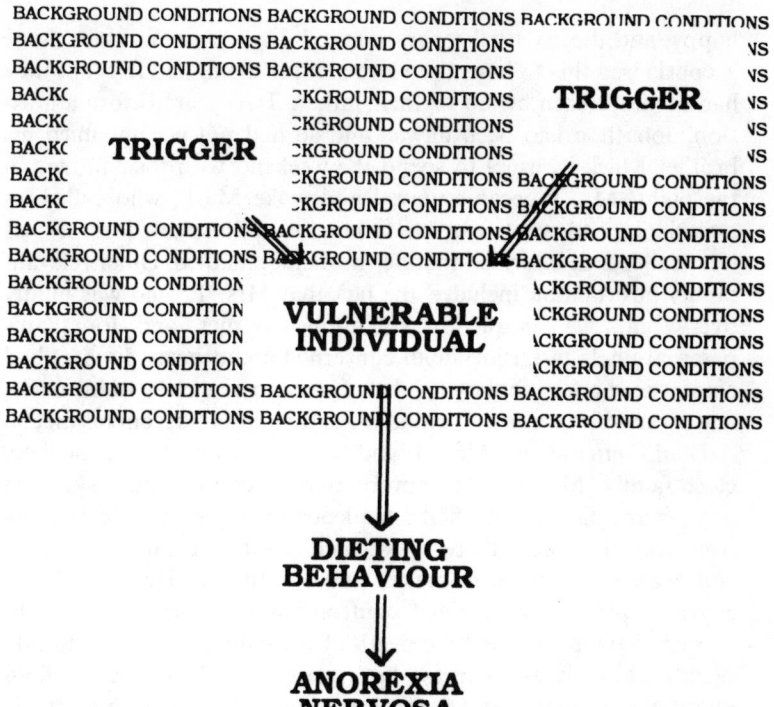

Figure 1 *Simplified aetiological model for anorexia nervosa*

school difficulties, etc., which are not related to sex in any way. This could be one of the reasons why the sex imbalance in anorexia nervosa, although still present in children, is less marked. The following case history may help to illustrate this.

CASE HISTORY - JONATHAN T
Jonathan was a thirteen year old boy referred to the eating disorders clinic following urgent admission to a paediatric ward. He was assessed and given a diagnosis of anorexia nervosa.

Family situation: Jonathan was the elder of two boys, both of whom lived at home with their mother following parental separation when Jonathon was 8. Their father had suffered from asthma, but had continued to smoke and drink heavily and he had died two years previously. He had been very devoted to his work and had often not been at home. The parents' marriage had not been happy, and the eventual separation and divorce acrimonious. Mrs. T considered this to have been stressful for them, and felt that they had at times been afraid of their father. Two years before admission, Jonathan had been unwell and so had not accompanied his brother Mark as usual to spend the weekend with their father. In the night, Mr. T became unwell and woke Mark, who called an ambulance and went with his father to the hospital. Mrs. T was later called and informed that her husband had died. Other relevant family information included the fact that Mrs. T, who was mildly overweight, was frequently attempting to diet, and Jonathan's paternal uncle (a businessman concerned about heart disease) had commenced a low cholesterol diet. Jonathan was close to his uncle, and aware of the reasons behind his cutting out fats from his diet.

Family interaction: Mrs. T and her sons formed an articulate, close family. Mrs. T was appropriately in control, but asked the boys their opinions. She had a tendency to err on the side of being overprotective, and there was some denial of family conflict. Jonathan was the peace-maker and negotiator. He was always eager to please and avoided confrontations. Whereas Mark appeared to have mourned the death of his father, being able to talk openly about it and express both positive and negative feelings about Mr. T, Jonathan was much more guarded on the subject. He did not express any negative emotions regarding his father.

Developmental and Medical History: Jonathan was born following two miscarriages. Mrs. T had been very anxious throughout the pregnancy. The birth was difficult following induction against Mrs. T's wishes. Birth weight was normal and Jonathan was a healthy baby who fed well. Developmental milestones were normal and he was described as contented and easy to comfort. There was no history of emotional or behavioural problems, with the exception of some obsessional tendencies. There was no history of feeding difficulties. He was described as a rather solitary child. There was nothing of apparent relevance in his medical history: he had suffered from hay fever in summer and occasional headaches. He had received no previous treatment for an eating disorder and had never been overweight.

History of presenting problems: Jonathan had from an early age had a tendency to become obsessed with certain interests. This started at the age of two with cartoon characters, and had progressed through film characters, pop singers, electronic music, and finally food and health. His mother recognised a pattern in these 'fads' which had always previously passed with time. However, the preoccupation with food and health, which had started three months prior to admission into the paediatric ward, and gradually intensified with increasing physical deterioration. Jonathan would check food for additives, and would refuse anything he thought might be harmful. He stuck rigidly to a 300 kcal per day diet. Each morning he got up at 6:30 am to run a mile before going to school, and each evening he ran a further two miles. When he began to panic about the possibility of missing his early morning run his mother sought medical advice. She had become worried about his poor state of health, and thought that he might be causing himself permanent physical damage. In the two weeks prior to admission, Jonathan had been in the middle of revision and examinations. He and his mother had negotiated a truce for this period, which involved his mother not mentioning food to him. Admission was precipitated by renal failure secondary to severe weight loss.

Physical and mental state on examination: On admission, he was extremely thin with evidence of generalised muscle wasting. His weight had dropped to 72% of the desired weight for his age and he was in the second of the five stages of pubertal development (Tanner et al., 1966). There was no evidence of overt depression, vomiting, laxative abuse or binge eating. Excessive exercising, fear of fatness and distortion of body image were all deemed to be present. The diagnosis of anorexia nervosa in a young adolescent male with obsessional tendencies was made.

If we look at the potentially relevant background and precipitating factors in this case the following emerge:

- parental separation and long history of animosity
- death of father, and circumstances thereof
- mother's continual attempts to diet and lose weight
- uncle's health concerns and fat-free diet
- school exam time

Clearly there may be other relevant factors, including those related to individual vulnerability such as Jonathan's tendency towards obsessionality, his difficulty dealing with negative emotions in general, etc. However, this case illustrates some of the themes we see regularly in children with anorexia nervosa, few of which are particularly sex specific. In Matthew's case mentioned earlier, potential precipitating factors included family move, a change in school (resulting in loss of friends) and his mother commencing an oligoantigenic diet for medical reasons. Finally, it is of interest to note that in many boys, the refusal of food and pronounced fear of becoming fat often seems to be linked to notions of health and fitness, rather with any notion of an ideal body shape. A number of boys presenting to our clinic have been particularly concerned with heart disease. For example, one twelve year old boy had become preoccupied with his own and his father's health and diet following the death of a school friend's father from heart disease.

CONCLUSION

It is proposed in this chapter that boys and young adolescent males can present with anorexia nervosa as defined by standard diagnostic criteria (ie. APA, 1987). Boys who develop such an eating disorder may show a variable illness course dependent on a whole range of different factors – as indeed is the case with females. Boys do not necessarily have a better or poorer prognosis by virtue of their sex alone. The fact that boys tend to form a greater percentage of the younger group of patients presenting for treatment of anorexia nervosa remains a subject of interest and one for which no conclusive reasons have been found. The suggestion has been put forward here that many of the commonly identified precipitating factors in children with anorexia nervosa are not sex specific. This combined with the naturally occurring heightened body sensitivity of individuals of both sexes entering and going through puberty, may account for the relatively higher proportion of males.

REFERENCES

American Psychiatric Association (1987) *Diagnostic and Statistical Manual of Mental Disorders 3rd Edition.* Washington, DC: APA

Bryant-Waugh R., Knibbs J., Fosson A., Kaminski Z. & Lask B. (1988) Long term follow up of patients with early onset anorexia nervosa. *Archives of Disease in Childhood*, 63: 5–9

Burns T. & Crisp A. H. (1984) Outcome of anorexia nervosa in males. *British Journal of Psychiatry*, 145: 319–325

Burns T. & Crisp A. H. (1985) Factors affecting prognosis in male anorexics. *Journal of Psychiatric Research*, 19: 323–328

Crisp A. H. & Burns T. (1983) The Clinical presentation of anorexia nervosa in males. *International Journal of Eating Disorders*, 2: 5–10

Crisp A. H., Burns T. & Bhat A. V. (1986) Primary anorexia nervosa in the male and female: A comparison of clinical features and prognosis. *British Journal of Medical Psychology*, 59: 123–132

Fichter M. M. & Daser C. (1987) Symptomatology, psychosexual development and gender identity in 42 anorexic males. *Psychological Medicine*, 17: 409–418

Fosson A., Knibbs J., Bryant-Waugh R. & Lask B. (1987) Early onset anorexia nervosa. *Archives of Disease in Childhood*, 62: 114–118

Hall A. , Delahunt J. W. & Ellis P. M. (1985) Anorexia Nervosa in the Male: Clinical features and follow-up of nine patients. *Journal of Psychiatric Research*, 19(2/3): 315–321

Hawley R.M. (1985). The outcome of anorexia nervosa in younger subjects. *British Journal of Psychiatry*, 146: 657–660

Herzog D.M, Norman D.K, Gordon C & Penpose M (1984). Sexual conflict and eating disorders in 27 males. *American Journal of Psychiatry*, 141: 989–994

Higgs J. F., Goodyear I. M. & Birch J. (1989) Anorexia Nervosa and Food Avoidance Emotional Disorder. *Archives of Disease in Childhood*, 64: 346–351

Jacobs B. W. & Isaacs S. (1986) Pre-pubertal anorexia nervosa: A retrospective controlled study. *Journal of Child Psychology and Psychiatry*, 27: 237–250

Kalucy R. S., Crisp A. H. & Harding B. (1977) A study of 56 families with anorexia nervosa. *British Journal of Medical Psychology*, 50: 381–395

Morgan H.G. & Russell G.F.M. (1975). Value of family background and clinical features as predictors of long term outcome in anorexia nervosa: four year follow-up study of 41 patients. *Psychological Medicine*, 5: 355–371

Nielsen S. (1990). The epidemiology of anorexia nervosa in Denmark from 1973 to 1987: a nationwide register study of psychiatric admission. *Acta Psychiatrica Scandinavia*, 81: 507 – 514

Slade P. (1982) Towards a functional analysis of anorexia nervosa and bulimia nervosa, *British Journal of Clinical Psychology*, 21: 167–179

Sterling J. W. & Segal J. D. (1985) Anorexia nervosa in males: A critical review. *International journal of Eating Disorders*, 4: 559- 572

Vandereycken W. & Van de Broucke S. (1984) Anorexia nervosa in males: A comparative study of 107 cases reported in the literature (1970 to 1980). *Acta Psychiatrica Scandinavia*, 70: 447–454

Notes on Contributors

Bridget Dolan has worked with people suffering with eating problems over the past ten years both in the Eating Disorders Clinic at St George's Hospital and at Henderson Hospital, a psychotherapeutic in-patient unit for women and men with personality disorders. She has a particular research interest in social and cultural aspects of disordered eating behaviour and has published several theoretical and research papers. She has carried out cross-cultural research into eating attitudes and behaviour in Poland, Nigeria and Egypt. In Britain she has researched into eating behaviours of women in various situations, including women in prison, in treatment units and in the general community. Bridget Dolan has co-ordinated the European Council of Eating Disorders since its establishment in 1989.

Inez Gitzinger is a psychoanalyst in training (DPV) at the Werner Schwidder Klinik of psychosomatic medicine and research fellow at the Center for Psychotherapy Research, Stuttgart. She has worked with women and men with eating disorders over the past eight years. She is one of the active members of the Multicentre Study on Eating Disorders in Germany. Her particular research interests are in personality (defences and coping) and in sexual abuse. She co-organised the *Why Women?* meeting at the University of Ulm, Germany, in 1990.

Karin Bell is a specialist in Internal Medicine and Psychoanalysis working in private practice since 1978. She was previously at the

Psychosomatic Department of Cologne University, as lecturer and didactic analyst since 1972. Karin has been Chair of the Deutsche Gesellschaft für Psychoanalyse, Psychotherapie, Psychosomatik und Tiefenpsychologie since 1992 and is a Member of the General Assembly of North Rhine Medical Chamber. Her previous publications consider issues in psychoanalytical education and theory and practice of psychoanalysis with emphasis on the problems of women.

Rachel Bryant-Waugh is Principal Clinical Psychologist and Co-ordinator of Eating Disorders Research at the Hospital for Sick Children, Great Ormond Street, London. She has over ten years' experience of working with children with eating disorders, and has contributed to both the clinical and research activity at Great Ormond Street Hospital. She currently leads a busy research team engaged in investigating various aspects of childhood onset eating disorders. In 1993 she co-edited a book on the subject, *Childhood Onset Anorexia Nervosa and Related Eating Disorders*, Lask, B. and Bryant-Waugh, R. (eds), Lawrence Erlbaum Associates Ltd.

Judith Bullerwell-Ravar, Docteur d'Etat in clinical psychology, works in private practice as a therapist and also teaches interpersonal communication at university level. Her research has been mainly concerned with body image and self-image of bulimics. One of the first therapists in France to specialise in the treatment of eating disorders, she helped set up the French equivalent of the Eating Disorders Association, the G.E.F.A.B., in 1984, and has been General Secretary of this association since that time.

Rachel Calam is Senior Tutor in Clinical Psychology at the University of Manchester. She has a background of work in child abuse and has worked with families for several years. She has a particular research interest in the way in which unwanted sexual experiences may contribute to the development of preoccupation with some aspect of the body, and to psychological disturbance more generally.

Pat Hartley is Reader in Health Studies at University College Salford. She has worked in the field of eating disorders since 1974, when she founded Anorexic Aid, the first self-help and support group for people with problems around food. Her other research interests include body image and self-esteem, education and prevention in relation to anorexia and bulimia nervosa.

Werner Köpp, M.D., is internist and psychoanalyst at the Department of Psychosomatic Medicine and Psychotherapy, at the Klinikum Steglitz der FU Berlin. He has worked with eating disordered patients over the past ten years. His particular research interest is the field of psychodynamic and psychoanalytic treatment of patients with eating disorders. He has carried out investigations about obesity, sexual abuse and treatment outcome.

Malcolm Laing is a Nurse Therapist who worked at the Cullen Centre, Department of Psychotherapy, Royal Edinburgh Hospital. He has worked with women and men with eating disorders for the past eight years and has developed an interest in working, in group situations, with people suffering from bulimia nervosa. He is currently working as a therapist in a medical centre in Leith, Edinburgh, and also has a private practice in central Edinburgh. He is a member of B.A.B.C.P.

Mary Levens has worked for the past ten years at the eating disorders unit of Atkinson Morley's Hospital, London, as a therapist and supervising the eating disorders team. She is qualified as a Psychodramatic Psychotherapist and Art Therapist; she writes widely on these topics and runs private training sessions for staff working in personality disorders and eating disorders.

Jenny Munro has been involved in eating disorders research in Edinburgh for four years. She is now working in a clinical setting and has a particular interest in group psychotherapy and self-help for women with eating disorders.

Sheila Ritchie works as a psychoanalytic psychotherapist with special responsibility for eating problems at the Women's Therapy Centre, London. She is a training member of the Association for Group and Individual Psychotherapy. She sees women individually and in groups and offers workshops in the area of body image and eating problems. She also trains professionals working in the field. For the last eighteen years the Women's Therapy Centre has developed an understanding of women's psychology from a feminist perspective acknowledging the impact of woman's social position on her internal world.

Maxine Rogers is a Freelance Illustrator. She has produced illustrations for books, magazines and newspapers. She has worked extensively for the *Observer* and *The Sunday Telegraph*. Her work naturally contains a humorous element; however, she is equally able to address serious issues with the appropriate visual impact.

Julie Shaw is a Lecturer in Social Sciences at Rotherham College of Arts and Technology. She is currently conducting her doctoral research into the media's influence upon the development and maintenance of eating problems.

Peter Slade is Professor of Clinical Psychology at Liverpool University. He has worked with women with eating problems for over twenty-five years, initially at the Maudsley and Royal Free Hospitals in London and then for the past sixteen years in Liverpool. He has carried out research work on body image problems, perfectionism and unwanted sexual experiences in women with eating disorders.

Rose Stockwell worked from 1980 to 1993 in specialist eating disorder settings with in-patient and out-patient treatments in the NHS as an occupational therapist and therapist. She is currently working in private practice as a psychotherapist. Many of her patients are working to reveal, understand and work through the issues that underlie, and at times are subsumed by, the symptoms and preoccupations of an eating disorder.

Ellie van Vreckem is a group and family therapist in the Eating Disorders Unit of U.C. St-Josef, Kortenberg, Belgium. She has worked with women with eating problems over the past twelve years and has a particular interest in sibling interactions in eating disordered families. She participates in several research projects about sexual trauma and dissociation and is interested in transgenerational issues in this field.

Walter Vandereycken is Professor of Psychiatry at the Catholic

University of Leuven. Head of the Department of Behaviour Therapy at the Alexian Brothers Psychiatric Hospital in Tienen and consultant psychiatrist at the University Psychiatric Centre in Kortenberg, Belgium, he has been intensively involved in treatment of and research into eating disorders over the past twenty years. He has published widely on this subject. His most recent book, *From Fasting Saints to Anorexic Girls: The History of Self-Starvation*, is also published by The Athlone Press (1994).

Glenn Waller is a Senior Lecturer in Clinical Psychology at the School of Psychology, University of Birmingham. He has worked clinically with women with eating disorders for the past six years. His research interests are in the area of the aetiology and mainten-ance of eating problems (including the roles of sexual abuse, the family, control, the media and ethnic factors) and in the cognitive processes underlying eating.

Winny Weeda-Mannak is a Research Fellow at the University of Amsterdam. She has been director of the research programme "Early detection of eating disorders: A prospective study in females aged 14–18 years in secondary schools", which is financed by the Praeventiefonds. She was previously director of the out-patient clinic for eating disorders at the Free University Hospital, Amster-dam. She has carried out research into aspects of early recognition of anorexia nervosa in those groups with an increased risk of developing anorexia nervosa.

Index

Index of Authors